THE BRASSERIES
OF PARIS

THE
BRASSERIES
of PARIS

By François Thomazeau

Photographs by Sylvain Ageorges

Translated by Anna Moschovakis

THE LITTLE BOOKROOM

NEW YORK

Library of Congress Cataloging-in-Publication Data

Thomazeau, François.
[Brasseries de Paris. English]
The brasseries of Paris / by François Thomazeau ; photos by Sylvain
Ageorges ; translated by Anna Moschovakis.
p. cm.
Includes bibliographical references and index.
ISBN-13: 978-1-892145-49-9 (alk. paper)
ISBN-10: 1-892145-49-9 (alk. paper)
1. Restaurants — France — Paris — Guidebooks. I. Title.
TX907.5.F72P37763 2007
647.950944'361--dc22   2007013425

Published by The Little Bookroom
1755 Broadway, 5th floor, New York NY 10019
editorial@littlebookroom.com • www.littlebookroom.com

Distributed in the U.S. by Random House, in the U.K. and
Ireland by Signature Book Services, and in Europe by
Random House International.

Contents

Introduction
THE BRASS IN BRASSERIE

T HESE DAYS, BRASSERIES BREW UP A BIT OF EVERYTHING, MINUS THE BEER, WHICH WAS THEIR ORIGINAL FUNCTION. *Brasser* is the French word for "brew," but it also has a secondary meaning: to mix. And while many an idea, business plan, and birthday celebration is brewed up in the contemporary brasserie, it's also a mixing place—for tourists and epicures, recipes and regions.

Brasseries are a real institution, a way of being Parisian, a safe haven for tradition—while at the same time they have very little to do with what they once were. As with bistro, pub, and cabaret, the very word has been renovated, updated to suit the times and better fit a new reality. For after all, what does a *"grande brasserie parisienne"* look like today? What are Lipp, Bofinger, Le Wepler, Le Zimmer, even Le Fouquet's...restaurants? Yes, but not exactly—they are both more and less than that. Cafés? Definitely, but big ones, and not at all times of the day...Canteens? Yes, sort of, but more chic...

Brasseries are always expansive, and all of the establishments counted within these pages cheerfully serve their standard two hundred tables per day. And, just as we've come to talk about "bistro food," we now refer to a "brasserie menu"—that is, a lighter version of the bigger, bolder, and pricier dishes served in "real" restaurants.

A brasserie is this, too: food, fast—but never fast food. And, over time, the spirit of the brasserie has developed its own architecture, its own decor. To pass muster, first you need a large dining room—Art Nouveau, preferably, or at least Art Deco.

So, the spirit of the brasserie is a bit of all these things: stained-glass windows from the Exposition Coloniale; Mucha-inspired, flower-motifed images of women in flowing robes; Japonica furniture from the École de Nancy; Alsatian-style inlaid boiserie; mirrors and chrome. It's a whole brouhaha of inspired, sometimes inebriated discussions. And the efficient dance—one part French can-can—of the waiters and waitresses dressed traditionally, in black uniforms with white aprons, walking confidently between tables with their overflowing trays. The dishes are classics: sauerkraut, of course; seafood platter; herring with potatoes and oil; even *l'oeuf mayo*. And then, the whole dynasty of soups, from fish to onion. And the famous breakfast for a rough morning…plain broth, or bouillon.

It must have begun there, with the *bouillon*. It's 1860, and a butcher named Pierre-Louis Duval has an idea—like a flash of genius—for an unbeatable marketing strategy: to serve complete, tasty meals, cheaply and in a pleasant surrounding, to the Parisian worker. A beer, a soup, a bouillon…With apologies to purists and traditionalists alike: that was the moment when Duval, unawares, invented the idea of cheap food for the masses that later would develop into the chains so intensely deplored by devout gourmets.

But the idea was such a good one, and his bouillon was so delicious, that very quickly, prices rose and—the high price of success—Parisian celebrities became regulars at Le Bouillon Duval on the avenue de l'Opéra. In fact, it was in this granddaddy of all brasseries that in 1893 an anarchist named Leauthier stabbed a "bourgeois" to death, simply because he was well-dressed and wore a decorated jacket. It was the ambassador of Serbia. Already, Duval had gone beyond serving the little people.

Then the brothers Chartier, Camille and Edouard, came along to pick up where Duval left off—without deviating from the initial vocation of the brasserie: quality, value, and efficiency. Is it an accident that, more than 110 years later, their *bouillon* on the rue du Faubourg-Montmartre still prospers, and still retains the inimitable spirit they created? Without a doubt, it was the Chartier brothers who invented the *ésprit brasserie*— that touch of a dining-hall atmosphere, with conversations bouncing off the mirrors and from table to table.

And more than a century ago—well before Clément, Hipoppotamus, and Léon de Bruxelles, the Chartier brothers invented the chain restaurant: Le Bouillon Racine, Le Montparnasse 1900, and the brasserie Vagenende all were Chartier establishments, until a reversal of the family fortune reduced them to eating…bouillon, and forced them to sell to their competitors, Vagenende and Rougeot.

Because Parisian brasseries are this, too: a tale of families, of rivalries, mergers and acquisitions, crossed fortunes, tough luck, sudden failures. Business, too, is brewed in the brasserie.

It's no different today. Jean-Paul Bucher, proprietor of the Flo brasseries, and the Blanc brothers split the lion's share of the city's business. It makes the independents' blood boil, the traditionalists cry out in protest. What? These brasseries, which passed long ago into the status of historical monuments, now in the service of chain-management, of business plans? In the wake of the two major players, Gérard Jouilie and the Costes brothers are attempting to gobble up the rest. With their fierce but polite competition, at least Flo and the Blanc brothers kept up the tradition of brasseries—they were still the real thing. But it turns out these two industry giants had eyes too big for their stomachs. Flo finally succumbed to a buyout by the Belgian billionaire, Albert Frère, while the Blanc brothers got gobbled up by a bank and trust. What will the purists say? At least Bucher and the Blancs got their start in the kitchen or on the floor. Only time will tell whether the brasserie will drown in a wave of globalization.

That term—as badly as it's been misinterpreted in Paris—had its own meaning in eastern France, the ancestral region of the Blanc brothers (sons of Moselle) and of Jean-Paul Bucher, a full-blooded Alsatian. In the same way that we owe our bistros to the Cossacks who rushed Paris at the tail-end of the nineteenth century and demanded in Russian to be served quickly (*"bistro"*), we owe our brasseries to the Prussians. It was the 1870 annexation of Alsace by Germany that forced some of the best cooks in the region, determined to remain French, to bring their sausages and their *kugelhopfs* to the capital.

The German Zimmers, the Alsatian Weplers, Zeyers, Bofingers, Lipps, Jennys: the names of these famous makers of sauerkraut, of pretzels and *gewurtz*, are to this day synonymous with good dining and good taste.

Alsatians are to brasseries what Auvergnats are to bistros: a tradition, a line, a culture, an *Appellation d'Origine Contrôlée*.

Here, too, the concept was such a winner that all the drinking holes in the capital which also served food soon dressed themselves up with the name, brasserie, which was as trendy at the turn of the last century as it is today to have a hamburger on the menu (to add a dash of youth) and a vegetarian plate (to add a morsel of conscientiousness). Or, to install a "lounge" where there once was a real salon.

The big, shiny brasseries in this little guide don't necessarily serve plentiful meals at all hours for next to nothing any more. Gentrification has won, and now the menus are written for diners with plenty in their purse. But the value-for-price equation is still remarkably good—as is the speedy, affable, and efficient service. Of course, we've all had one of those dining experiences when everything goes wrong—a broken dish, an interminable wait, politeness relegated to the back burner—only to dine divinely in the same brasserie a few weeks later. The restaurant business—especially at one thousand customers a day—is not an exact science. And the best of these refectories of the last century have all but immersed themselves in a bygone era when life was not set aside for the sake of mere nutrition—when the pleasures of the eye were part and parcel of the pleasures of the table.

Each with its own soul, its own cachet, its legends large and small, its ghosts—famous or less so—that send shivers down backs when they rattle the kitchen door: brasseries rustle with all that makes Parisian life Parisian. Celebrated meeting points for journalists (La Closerie and La Coupole); for theater artists (Le Zimmer, Le Procope); of writers, tourists, elderly couples, of "the people." They are, in a sense, the Belly of Paris.

In homage to Bottin, the famous writer of belles lettres who frequented their booths religiously, the self-respecting brasserie will establish a literary prize: Lipp has one, as do La Closerie, Vaudeville, Wepler, Fouquet's…. Innovators in 1900, brasseries have since then formed an integral part of the Parisian landscape, of its heritage and its habits—a bit like the role of the giant dining halls of Vienna or Prague.

Are their quality and authenticity under threat? No more than those of other hallmark establishments in the city. Flo and the Blanc brothers built their empires without any honest critic noticing a decline in service or cuisine. And the fact that they have been bought up by larger investors suggests that the concept is still worth believing in. At the same time, the independents resist with greater strength, convinced that their establishments provide that extra dose of originality and soul, which can at times be missing from certain of the chain brasseries, whose reliable but uniform quality might finally be their weak link.

As for the spirit of the *bouillon*, it has vanished already… and brasseries are now for the most part establishments for the better-off, a bit too posh for workers or students. But, in an era of fast food, of salads eaten with your hands, of themed chain restaurants for which absolute uniformity is a creed, brasseries still manage an important task: the combination of speed and quality, variety and tradition.

Au Chien qui Fume

33, RUE DU PONT-NEUF, 1ST ARR.

☏ 01 42 36 07 42   🚇 LES HALLES

OPEN DAILY FROM NOON UNTIL 2:00AM

THE SMOKING DOG; NOW HERE IS A BUSINESS NAME THAT SEEMS UNLIKELY TO PLEASE THE AMERICAN TOURIST: What's this? A dog in a restaurant? And a smoking one, to boot? But not to worry. There are dozens of smoking dogs at the Chien qui Fume, but they have never bitten anyone—not even the painters who drew their portraits so they could be mounted on the walls of one of the oldest restaurants in Paris. The origin of the name, though, is the subject of

some controversy: in the most official version of the legend, it derives from the four-legged companion of a former proprietor. It's a fine bone to chew on for the patrons of this much-frequented establishment, a fixture in the neighborhood of Les Halles since 1740. But we don't feel any great desire to dispel the mystery. Why not the smoking dog, after all? The name possesses enough poetry that it was able to provide inspiration for André Breton one evening as he passed by the restaurant: "Torpors spread like

steam / at the Chien qui Fume / where pro and con had just walked in"
["Sunflower"]. An excellent point of entry into a matter of some debate: is
the Chien qui Fume a brasserie at all? Against it, there is the fact that this
dog already was smoking—in a café—long before brasseries came into
fashion. In its favor are its size, its indubitable status as an institution, and the
casual way it thumbs its nose at the equally animal Pied de Cochon, across
from it in Les Halles. There's also the lively banter of the waitstaff and
the classic presentation of the cuisine—seafood platters, excellent smoked
salmon *à la maison*, breast of lamb, *marmite de lotte*, or the extravagant
prix fixe menu *Chien coquin*, which encourages diners to indulge.

Au Pied de Cochon

6, RUE COQUILLIERE, 1ST ARR.

☎ 01 40 13 77 00   🚇 LES HALLES

OPEN DAILY 24 HOURS

THIS IS WHERE IT ALL BEGAN FOR THE BLANC BROTHERS. THIS FORMER BASTION OF THE OFFICIAL PARIS MARKET at Les Halles seemed destined to become a butcher shop, but instead

became a brasserie—and, before too long, an institution. Too big at first for the limited commerce in the area, the Pied de Cochon soon turned into a blessing for the Blanc family, a ground-floor entrée into a booming new trend. The founder of the dynasty, *pater familias* Clément Blanc (who would later bestow his first name on the chain of restaurants that built a fortune for the company founded by his sons), bought the building just after the War and conferred its operation on his sister, the famed Madame Ott,

who reigned over her little universe for half a century. Almost immediately the establishment transformed itself into a hotspot for Parisian nightlife. Many a weary night-trawler loved—and still loves—to come here for the famous onion soup, which will help sooth the spirit at 5am, as Paris awakes. The first revelers to frequent this place didn't see pink elephants but were likely to cross paths with Oscar, a pig made of flesh (primarily) and blood (incidentally), all gussied up and perfumed, which Madame Ott would parade through the crowd back in the days when the brasserie was just establishing its foothold in the neighborhood.

Its location was certainly ideal, here in the "Belly of Paris," as it devolved first into a meat market and then into a debauch of tourists, restless youth, and commercialization. We may never know what became of Oscar, but the pig's feet you can still order at the Pied de Cochon are worth the detour. For those with smaller appetites, we'd recommend the equally succulent *pied farci*, accompanied by a fruity Beaujolais.

Chez Flottes

2, RUE CAMBON, 1ST ARR.

☎ 01 42 60 80 89   🚇 CONCORDE

OPEN DAILY FROM 11:30AM UNTIL 1:00AM

ANY LINGERING FEARS THAT THE *ÉSPRIT BRASSERIE* HAS GONE OUT OF STYLE ARE ROUNDLY CRUSHED BY CHEZ FLOTTES, an establishment that has figured out how to marry—subtly and tastefully—modernity with tradition, earthiness with innovation, and respect for the past with faith in the future.

Founded in 1966 by the Flottes family, the restaurant that bears its name is, at forty, young for a brasserie. Olivier Flottes imported the best of his native Aveyron—the *aligot*, which is light, delectable, and omnipresent; a juicy *viande de Salers*, perfectly cooked; *confit* that melts in your mouth—not to mention the  traditional hospitality and *savoir vivre* so dear to Paris' Auvergnats. The decor fits squarely into the lineage of old-fashioned brasseries—floral stained-glass, *femmes-fleurs*, ornate glass centerpiece—without descending into retro kitsch.

In fact, in this quiet and private spot—tucked away behind the Champs-Elysées, Chez Flottes has

been able to preserve some of the spirit of the bistro (an Auvergnian invention), and you'll be tempted to have lunch at the handsome old-style zinc counter in the company of a staff that is efficient, enthusiastic, and always friendly. The small army in charge of the dining room is a bit like the one at Mélac; they wear modernized *rondins* (the item worn around the belly into which they tuck money), with STAFF stamped on the back, reassuring tourists without turning their back on this century.

The wine selection is judicious, the seafood is delicious, and this near-flawlessness has made Chez Flottes a food critic's darling. And that's not all: the prices aren't inflated and the mood is always jovial—a real rarity, just steps from the place de la Concorde, with its paradises of deluxe artifice and its tourists by the busload.

Zimmer

1, PLACE DU CHÂTELET, 1ST ARR.

☎ 01 42 36 74 03   🚇 CHATELET

OPEN DAILY FROM 7AM UNTIL 2AM (12:30 ON SUNDAY)

NUMBER 1, PLACE DU CHÂTELET: A BETTER ADDRESS IS HARD TO IMAGINE. THE CARS ZIP ROUND IN THE HUSTLE and bustle of the *place*, but the Zimmer is strangely calm, protected from the tumult by a row of trees, placed shoulder to shoulder along the edges of the Théatre du Châtelet, to which the Zimmer is annexed. When it opened, in fact, people flowed freely from one to the other—from theater to restaurant, from food for the mind to food for the body, simply by walking through a door.

From a seat on the terrace, you won't get the showy decor (very *grand-siècle*) of the main dining room, recently updated in a hybrid modernist-classical style by Jacques Garcia, but you will catch a glimpse of the Sarah-Bernhardt (a bar named after the famous actress who used to play regularly at the Châtelet) out of the corner of your eye. And Sarah Bernhardt herself is only the beginning of the long list of the Zimmer's famous patrons: Jules Verne, Richard Strauss, Gustav Mahler, Toscanini, Claude Debussy, Émile Zola, Marcel Proust, Guillaume Apollinaire, Nijinsky, Edmond Rostand, Toulouse-Lautrec, Pablo Picasso, Igor Stravinsky, even Céline…. It is an historic place, without a doubt. And the elderly couples, the well-dressed businessmen, the well-heeled tourists and theatergoers who gather there form a visibly upscale clientele. The menu, though, is far from reaching the elevated prices of certain other similarly lofty institutions. And the selection of light and varied appetizers, as well as the nods to vegetarians and to diners whose tastes tend toward the exotic, are proof that the contemporary, too, has earned its place at the table.

Discrete speakers hung from the solid, carved-stone columns diffuse tasteful blues recordings, perhaps a subtle homage to the activists of May 1968 who once gathered here, working to forge a new world in this symbol of the old one. But tradition never fully cedes its place, and in the tender flesh of the munster, in the subtly spicy aroma of cumin, all of Alsace is right there, at the end of your fork.

Although it's situated smack in the center of the city, the Zimmer has a secret charm to it. Rumors persist that, concealed in a basement three flights below ground level, members of the Resistance used to hide. Who can say for sure?

When, at rush hour, the dining room explodes in a sudden frenzy, it's reminiscent of the grand époque, of those manic years when the brasserie was comprised of four stories and dozens of professions: hunters, servers, firemen, a washerwoman… and so on.

Gallopin

IS THERE A SINGLE BEER-DRINKER FROM FRANCE OR THE NAVARRE WHO IS AWARE THAT TO ORDER A *GALLOPIN* IS automatically to pay tribute to Gustave Gallopin, the founder of one of the oldest and most stylish brasseries in all of Paris?

On September 1, 1876, at 40, rue de Notre-Dame-des-Victoires, the man in question opened a retail beer-and-wine shop that is now an institution of the place de la Bourse. In the beginning, Gallopin sold small servings of beer (20 cl instead of the 25 cl in the usual small glass), poured into silver mugs to keep them chilled. Some 130 years later, the tradition continues.

And silver—or money, in any case—is one of the most popular topics of conversation in this intimate, English-style brasserie, which attracted a clientele of stockbrokers after the trading floor had closed. Big gains were celebrated with champagne, and every afternoon a zinc tub filled with bottles gave the lucky ones the chance to pop a cork or two. The

less fortunate could always settle for a *gallopin*.

After his own fortune was made, Gallopin bought up the two shops next to his own and his establishment grew into one of the most frequented in Paris. The "grand bar," painstakingly carved in Cuban ebony by the best woodworkers, soon welcomed the elite of the Corbeille. The lower-level traders, legal representatives, and agents filled up at the "petit bar," and the clerks hung out at "42" (along with those who'd lost their shirts).

The spectacular 1900 room, with its expansive stained-glass window, was completed for the Universal Expo and still reverberates with the spiciest anecdotes of the palais Brongniart (even if the French stock market has since gone virtual). You'll still find traders—journalists, too—whispering together in the rays of sunlight that filter in through the colored glass. In the triangle formed by Le Grand Colbert, Le Vaudeville, and Le Gallopin, the last is the coziest, the most muted of the three business-district brasseries.

After several changes in ownership, in 1997 the restaurant passed into the hands of the Alexandres (formerly of Bofinger) and, now, into those of their son Sebastien. But a jolt of youthfulness has changed nothing about the special atmosphere of the place: not its traditional cuisine (trusted since then to a former chef from La Coupole), nor the discreet friendliness of the wait staff, nor the beauty of the women walking through its doors. They come at night now as well, after an evening at the theater— though for a very long time the Gallopin was only open for lunch.

Le Grand Colbert

2, RUE VIVIENNE, 2ND ARR.

☏ 01 42 86 87 88   🚇 BOURSE

OPEN DAILY FROM NOON UNTIL 1:00AM

WINDING BETWEEN THE RUE VIVIENNE, THE *PASSAGE* OF THE SAME NAME, AND THE RUE DES PETITS-CHAMPS, Le Grand Colbert is a brasserie of the shadows. Whether you enter by way of the gallery and dine *en terrasse* beneath the stained-glass window, which gives a pleasant, aquarium-like aspect to this wing of the restaurant, or by way of rue Vivienne, into the muted shade penetrated here and there by rays of light from the sun or from the tall standing lamps, it's an atmosphere that inspires intimacy. Which is unusual for such a vast room with seating for a hundred, with ceilings perched at a height of six meters, with walls decorated in many-hued frescoes... Could it be the

panels of frosted glass, which insulate more than they separate; or the lighting, which is so evocative of the oil-lamps or candelabras of the great century into which the place was born? This is a brasserie for a quiet dinner for two, much more than for a celebratory night out after the rugby match.

Could it be, also, the shadows that haunt this place, which was renovated

30

more than children during the eighteenth century? Unless it's the hushed gossip of the ladies who would go shopping in the "novelty" shop that was erected—the first of its kind—during the reign of Louis-Phillipe, and under the sign of the Grand Colbert…

Or you may prefer to sit quietly in the back of the room on the gallery side, to partake from afar in the spectacle of the place—the celebrities who stop in from time to time to unwind after a show at one of the neighboring theaters, La Michodière and Les Variétés—as you partake of the soft light reflecting off the stained glass.

The tasteful, unaffected cuisine is supervised by Joël Fleury, the cheerful master chef and a dead ringer for the photographer Jean-Marie Périer. The menu, which is as classic as the decor, is reassuring and restrained.

Le Vaudeville

29, RUE VIVIENNE, 2ND ARR.

☎ 01 40 20 04 62   🚇 BOURSE, GRANDS-BOULEVARDS

OPEN DAILY FROM 7:00AM UNTIL 1:00AM

IT'S NO LONGER THE LOCAL CANTEEN FOR STOCKBROKERS, SINCE THE OLD TRADING FLOOR AT LA CORBEILLE IN THE palais Brongniart hasn't been in use for years, but Le Vaudeville has lost nothing for the change. This restaurant has seen its fair share of restructurings, bankruptcies…beginning with that of the theater that gave it its name. Imagine—it was here that, in 1852, *The Lady of the Camellias* had its stage debut! But a whole string of directors couldn't keep the theater afloat on applause alone; the 1300-seat establishment went under seven times during its brief forty years of existence.

The current incarnation of Le Vaudeville continues in the artistic tradition of its location by awarding an annual literary prize to a work that deviates from the beaten path. The brasserie, for its part, has not cut loose its anchors, keeping one eye on the place de la Bourse which has been handed over to young kids on roller skates (and to all manner of collectors and antiques merchants), and the other eye on the headquarters of the Agence France Presse, which provides it with loyal clients, stopping by on their way home from a day in the field or before taking off for the latest global hotspot.

Once upon a time, it was also a temple for coachmen and, later, cabbies, who would wait by the stock exchange for their wealthy clients. Epicures

only need apply.

One of Le Vaudeville's crowning jewels is its terrace, which is carefully partitioned by flower-filled planters, and where seats are so highly prized in summertime that the game of getting one rises nearly to the level of insider trading. The bar serves as a refuge for those waiting for a table—or maybe just for better days, for Le Vaudeville is one of the rare brasseries, dear to our hearts, where it's still permissible to order just a coffee or an aperitif.

Alongside reminders of the olden days—an elegant young woman checking coats and selling cigarettes from a wicker basket—those looking for a more frenetic atmosphere crowd into the *salle Art Deco*, with marble-work and lighting designed in 1927 by the Solvet brothers. Reflected in a jumble in the wide, beveled mirrors are the laughs and anecdotes of competing brokers, the scribes of *Le Nouvel Observateur*, the whispered tips of the dashing traders, or the gossip of the artistic directors from the record company that has settled on the *place*.

As for the cuisine, Le Vaudeville is owned by the Flo group, so there's nothing to fear; we have a weakness for the cod in *beurre blanc* sauce, with an accompanying glass of Tokay.

Chez Jenny

39, BOULEVARD DU TEMPLE, 3RD ARR.

☎ 01 44 54 39 00   🚋 REPUBLIQUE

OPEN DAILY FROM NOON UNTIL 1:00AM

YOU CAN'T CALL ROBERT JENNY A FORERUNNER: BOFIN-
GER AND FLODERER CAME BEFORE HIM AND SHOWED HIM
the way. In each case, an international expo provided the opportunity for
these Alsatian soldiers of good taste to bring their know-how and their
regional specialties to Parisians.

In the case of Robert Jenny, it was the Colonial Expo in 1931 that
gave him the chance to become the owner and operator of the brasserie
that bears his name: at the time he kept a modest kiosk where he sold
beer, sausage, and sauerkraut on the boulevard du Temple—the infa-
mous "boulevard of crime," so baptized because of its countless theaters
presenting risqué entertainment. The kiosk's success allowed its Stras-
bourgian owner to purchase the dining room of the old Victor ballroom—
which had been a Belgian restaurant, and a Russian one before that.

The Alsatian menu provided better results, despite the fact that four
years after the brasserie opened in 1932, Jenny sold the business to
Jean-Baptiste Fleck—another Alsatian, and the president of the Alsatian
hoteliers association, who in turn passed the reins to another compatriot,
Charles Bayer, in 1939.

In addition to a strictly Alsatian cuisine—sauerkraut, *cervelas*, *munster
au cumin*, *presskopf*—these three early proprietors also imposed a decor

typical of the fatherland of Parisian brasseries, accomplished at the hands of Charles Spindler, a known master of inlaid work (who was also working on the design of Bofinger). The wooden panels, first completed by an Alsatian company and installed for a century in the Saint-Leonard abbey, at the foot of Mount Sainte-Odile, remain an incomparable attraction of the expansive dining room, which looms over the place de la Republique.

Next, Jenny was turned over to Miroslav Siljegovic, owner of Le Flore and La Closerie des Lilas, before finally landing in the purse of the Blanc brothers, who had the excellent idea to alter it only by way of addition—of an adjoining Café Jenny, which attracts a younger, less formal crowd.

If, in the world of the brasserie, the Blanc brothers have become the gatekeepers of Alsace Lorraine, this address may be the best of all of theirs for sauerkraut—especially the *choucroute au champagne*.

Bofinger

IF LE PROCOPE CAN BE CONSIDERED THE SENIOR DOYEN OF THIS GUIDE, OPENING THE DOOR FOR A GENERATION OF brasseries without even knowing it, the real pioneer of Paris' Alsatian brasserie is without a doubt Bofinger, tucked into this nook of the Bastille, protected from the frequent demonstrations, the traffic, and the storms of history. Everyone who drinks a glass of draft beer in Paris owes a nod to Frédéric Bofinger, who was the first in the city to serve beer on tap—in 1870, six years after opening his modest Alsatian shop, from which he also sold regional pork products. This child of Colmar met with instant success, and his brasserie continued to expand. Some elements of his 1880 decor have survived, despite numerous renovations effected by the four generations of owners who followed him.

After the First World War, Bofinger—at the time directed by the founder's son-in-law Albert Bruneau, and his associate Louis Barraud— swallowed up three adjacent storefronts in order to enlarge and improve its setting. The highlight of the new decor—entrusted to the architect Legay and interior decorator Mittgen and completed in 1921—is still the grand, floral-motif oval cupola, which sets off a stained-glass effigy of King Gambrinus ("the patron saint of beer") signed by the artists, Nerer and Royer. And it still draws crowds: some customers make reserva-

41

tions days in advance, just so they can play the part of *les immortels* in this illustrious academy of beer and pretzels. In lieu of storks, they sidle up to beautiful ceramic herons, handiwork of the sculptor Clément Massier.

The 1931 Colonial Expo and its influx of visitors inspired the managers to make some new additions to the decor. They appealed to the painter Jean-Jacques Walts (who went by the name Hansi), to rethink the brasserie's look—in 1982 the facade was returned to its 1919 appearance—and to create, on the second floor, the extravagantly pretty *salon Hansi*, where those seeking a more intimate ambiance can find refuge.

This was the era when Bofinger became a bastion of Parisian politics, of which it was said that governments could be made or unmade over a

plate of sauerkraut. But among the regulars, the intensity of debate reached its pinnacle one day in 1996, when the oldest brasserie in Paris was acquired by Jean-Paul Bucher. Ten years later, Bofinger has recovered its tranquil animation, the elegant dance of *"garçons"* on the winding stairway under the cupola, the scent of sauerkraut—a hundred orders are served each day—or of seafood. Eight hundred people served daily...and Bofinger has earned the honor of being one of the rare brasseries in all of Paris where it seems impossible to be unpleasantly surprised. With the return of chef Georges Belondrade, the fish dishes are more than ever given pride of place, but the sauerkraut remains a must. Across the way, the Petit Bofinger is a way to try the delectable fare of the main establishment at a more modest price.

43

Brasserie de l'Île-Saint-Louis

55, QUAI DE BOURBON, 4TH ARR.

☎ 01 43 54 02 59 🚇 PONT-MARIE, CHATELET, HÔTEL-DE-VILLE

OPEN DAILY EXCEPT WEDNESDAY, FROM NOON UNTIL MIDNIGHT

WE MIGHT ALMOST CATCH OURSELVES—WITHOUT WISHING ANY MISFORTUNE ON OUR CONTEMPORARIES, OF COURSE— hoping that the curse of the Pont-Rouge, the old bridge that led to the Île-St-Louis, might strike again, to preserve this oasis of good taste from the ocean of tourists that is submerging the heart of historic Paris. The Pont-Rouge has more or less completely collapsed six times, to the point where it's no longer worth trying to fix it but the Brasserie de l'Île-Saint-Louis has survived like a charm.

Simplicity is inscribed in the history of the place: more than a century ago, when it was the Taverne du Pont-Rouge, it set up a terrace facing

the Seine, which is still one of the coziest in the city. For a brief moment it answered to the name "L'Oasis"; at the time it was owned by a certain Lauer, a true-blue Alsatian who served sauerkraut, sausage, and beer to a bohemian clientele, no doubt in pursuit of the ghost of Baudelaire.

One evening in 1953 Paul Guépratte, the head chef for the

44

Duchess of Windsor (whose Parisian *pied-à-terre* was just steps away),
learned that Lauer was throwing in the towel. The deal was sealed with a
handshake across the wooden bar, which to this day supports an elaborate
coffee machine from a distant era. Two generations later a different
Paul Guépratte watches over the cash register, while his mother and
grandmother dine on blanquette with small glasses of champagne in the
almost maritime glimmer of a winter lunch.

A family affair…joined by a clientele of regulars. Liz Taylor and
Natalie Wood once dined here with Richard Burton and Peter O'Toole.
Brigitte Bardot felt so at home here that she once offered the proprietor's

wife a little dog named Baby. And the famous vegetarian seemed not to reproach the delicious meat that can be tasted here, at ageless long wooden tables, surrounded by eternally stylish red velvet.

The two dining rooms, with their ocher mosaic floors and ceilings painted *café-crème*, are bathed in a soft glow reflecting up from the Seine. It's warm and bright in the late morning, and dramatically dappled in the early-evening *heure de l'apéro*, the French cocktail hour.

Time passes, but nothing really changes. The brasserie was once also called the Café des Sports. A photograph of Gavin Hastings serves as a reminder that this is a big rugby spot. When the *XV au Chardon* (that's the French nickname for Scotland's rugby team) come to confront the *Coq Gaulois*, swarms of kilts descend upon the Île, making the walls reverberate with their chants. Year after year, sauerkraut after *cassoulet*, Reisling after Chablis, match after match, the family grows.

Brasserie Balzar

49, RUE DES ÉCOLES, 5TH ARR.

☎ 01 43 54 13 67   🚇 CLUNY-LA SORBONNE, SAINT-MICHEL

OPEN DAILY FROM NOON UNTIL MIDNIGHT

No DOUBT BECAUSE OF THE REBELLIOUS SPIRIT OF THE NEIGHBORING SORBONNE, THE BALZAR MAY BE THE ESTABlishment whose acquisition by Jean-Paul Bucher incurred the most wrath. Thirty years after May 1968, an activist group was actually formed—in 1998, year of the Parisian World Cup—to protest the fall of this Latin Quarter monument to the Flo conglomerate. As if the revolutionaries of old were to mount their last battle here, proving that by staging their reinvention of the world at the Balzar, it had been altered forever.

The mini-brasserie on the rue des Écoles, in any case, had long ago lost any resemblance to a student café. Camus and Sartre argued there about responsibility; literature lecturers and medicine students sat side by side at the tables. But ever since the decline of Saint-Germain-des-Prés, celebrities are more likely to be spotted in the crowd than students on stipends. It's already been fifteen years since the arrival of Vaclav Havel—who had gone from making political theater to a life of politics—was greeted by passionate cheers. But the most recent icon to challenge the place's hallowed history was Madonna, when she sat down on the terrace with Jean-Paul Gaultier.

Eight years after Balzar became a protectorate of Flo, the tension has relaxed. Nothing fundamental has changed in this place where editors and intellectuals meet, especially not the decor, which seems so immutable it's easy to wonder whether its existence didn't precede its essence, as Sartre would put it.

The precise date when Amedée Balzar—a likable, bearded giant —opened his establishment is also the subject of debate. It happened sometime between 1890 and 1897, in any case. But the age-old complicity between foaming beer and fomenting ideas quickly transformed this tavern into the beating heart of student life.

In 1931, Marcelin Cazes bought the business to turn it into a petit Lipp—younger and less posh than his brasserie at the other edge of the quarter. As he had there, he entrusted the renovations to the architect Madeline. And almost instantly, a little brother emerged, with the same dark woodwork, the same mirrors reflecting the blasé expressions of

regulars, the same velvet, the same tile work—and the same faithfulness
to a compact but trustworthy menu.

In 1961, Cazes handed it off, and it was May 1968 that re-launched the
business. The Balzar did, it must be said, have a front-row seat at the show.
Later a Basque man named Jean-Pierre Egurreguy took up the torch,
retaining chef Pierre Sauvet and his classic dishes—leeks vinaigrette,
oeufs mayo, and steak tartare—which withstand the tests of both time
and fashion. Ever since, the fires have been kept by Christian René, who
quotes Paul Bocuse's nouvelle cuisine without copying it.

Marty

20, AVENUE DES GOBELINS, 5TH ARR.

☎ 01 43 31 39 51   🚇 LES GOBELINS

OPEN DAILY FROM NOON UNTIL 11:00PM

D INNERS AT MARTY LEAVE BEHIND THE MEMORY OF GRAPE-FRUIT: A SINFULLY DELICIOUS FRUIT *PÂTE MAISON*, AND A glass of white Bordeaux the citrus low note so full and round it's criminal. Because Marty is an establishment built on subtleties, out of which the cuisine and the piquant charm build, crescendo-like, as does the space itself, laid out in a series of small levels, in which diners are never far from each other, but also never on top of each other. A convivial intimacy. And the service, in keeping with the ambiance, is discreet and never overbearing.

Is Marty a brasserie? Yes, because of its dimensions first and foremost, but also because of its muted respect for tradition, its taste for innovation, its concern for the client's appetite as well as his comfort.

In the song, "San Francisco," Maxime Le Forestier sang about a blue house with its back to the hill ("*une maison bleue, adossée à la colline*"); Marty is a *maison bleue* that's had its back to les Gobelins since 1913. It was once a hangout for coachmen, like

La Closerie or Le Vaudeville (good points of reference). *Maison bleue* because of its first initial, M; because of the planters filled with flowers lining its entryway; because of the informal wall-hangings within. Mahogany frames provide the nautical ambiance that you would expect from the oyster bar; the bar itself is rather clean-lined, paneled in wengé and sycamore since the 1930s. Photographs of the founders—Étienne Marty, mustachioed and robust, and his wife Marthe, a woman of character—are aging as well as the business.

A stalwart neighborhood institution, risking the no-man's land between La Mouffe and Montparnasse, Marty has a grand ship-like quality to it, and its seafood offerings should be the first you set your scope on. Outstanding *saint-jacques*, prawn ravioli, *fruits de mer* aplenty—chef Thierry Colas inflects his sea-borne menu with finesse. To say nothing of the grapefruit *pâte*!

Bouillon Racine

BOUILLON REMAINS A SPECIALTY AT THIS BEAUTIFUL ESTABLISHMENT WHICH, UP TO NOW, HAS NEVER BROUGHT any luck to its string of proprietors. And yet it was a jewel in the crown of the Chartier group soon after its 1905 opening; Camille, one of the two brothers, almost immediately nicknamed it the "Grand Bouillon" when he ordered it renovated in 1907—following the dictates of Art Nouveau—by architect Jean-Michel Bouvier and decorator Louis Trezel, who was already at work on Julien.

Starting with the jutting facade that covers the two floors of the restaurant, Bouvier experimented with boiseries, and with the effects of mirrors, typical of all the Chartier brasseries. Inside, the play of light, which dances upon Trezel's irises and hollyhocks, gives the main dining room its particular glow.

And then, like so many of its ilk, the Grand Bouillon fell prey to the passing years—left behind by the changing fashions, by the wars, and the financial woes of the Chartiers. While it didn't disappear, it did mutate into a canteen for the Sorbonne staff, managed by the administration without enthusiasm, despite its landmark status.

It had nearly been completely abandoned by 1996, when Belgian chef Olivier Simon, who was already well known around Paris, decided to restore

some grandeur to this *bouillon*. For several years, the Bouillon Racine was given new life and became an embassy of fine Belgian taste in Paris. Waterzoi, Trappist beers—the formula seemed to work—even more so after France Culture selected it as the setting for a regular show called "Bouillon de Culture," which covered topics of societal change in France.

But Olivier Simon went on to open a seafood annex next to the main restaurant, and it wasn't as successful as expected. And so now Luc Morand, a son of the Chamonix family which has run the brasserie L'M (a favorite for sports enthusiasts) for generations, has entered into the

adventure of running this magical, but difficult, place. True to his mountain origins (and to our own), Morand puts the emphasis on modest, earthy, and eternal dishes: onion soup, roast chicken. So what if the restaurant has a rocky past—why make a mountain of it?

Brasserie Lipp

151, BOULEVARD SAINT-GERMAIN, 6TH ARR.

☎ 01 45 48 53 91   🚇 SAINT-GERMAIN-DES-PRÉS

OPEN DAILY FROM NOON UNTIL 2:00AM

WHEN YOU ENTER THE LIPP FOR THE FIRST TIME, YOU MIGHT BE TEMPTED TO ASK, "IS THIS ALL?" AND THEN, little by little you are won over by the subtle magic of the place, and you understand why the visitor's book of this most posh of Parisian brasseries could easily fill two volumes of *Who's Who*.

Lipp has its customs, its traditions, its legends. One of the incongruities of the place is that it's easier to get a quiet seat in the back than it is to be seated up front, on the covered terrace near the entrance where people can see as well as be seen— let alone in the "bus," the room reserved for the real VIPs. Not to worry…you'll see. These days, television stars outnumber poets and politicians—but at the Lipp, the times hardly change any more quickly than the menu.

Ready for a quick cast of characters? Jacques Chirac, François Mitterand, Valéry Giscard d'Estaing, Georges Pompidou—

virtually every president of the fifth Republic—and Léon Blum too, all came by habitually, no doubt seduced by the classic and efficient arrangement of tables, where everyone sits side by side, and face to face, in an obligatory but discreet conviviality. The Lipp's reputation has also been sealed by the nobility of the literati: Proust, Gide, Saint-Exupéry, Hemingway, Camus, Malraux, even Léon-Paul Fargue, who was literally part of the decoration— his father, Léon, was responsible for the floral ceramics in one of the dining rooms.

As the house poet wrote in his book *The Pedestrian of Paris*, the "Lipp is an indispensable part of the Parisian landscape. Is it not the only place where for the price of a beer one can get a faithful and complete recapping of a day in French politics or letters?"

Did Léonard Lipp know he'd be founding an institution when in 1880 he opened his brasserie, Les Bords du Rhin, across from the church of Saint-Germain-des-Prés? It was the Auvergnat dynasty, the Cazes, which turned 151, boulevard Saint-Germain into Paris' favorite canteen. Marcelin Cazes, who started out delivering baths to people's homes (carrying a tub and small cistern on his back), took the helm from 1920 until he opened up the Balzar; he was succeeded by the legendary Roger Cazes, keeper of the famous *livre d'or*—that *Who's Who* filled with the names of his clientele.

The understated circa-1900 design, the classic and unerring menu (our weakness is for the *pied de porc farci* and *cervelas mayonnaise*), the selective familiarity of the waiters have made Lipp a rarefied destination, but also a democratic one—the prices are no steeper than in many establishments that are far more obscure.

La Closerie des Lilas

171, BOULEVARD DU MONTPARNASSE, 6TH ARR.

☎ 01 40 51 34 50   🚇 VAVIN

OPEN DAILY FROM NOON UNTIL 1:00AM

WHO WOULD BELIEVE IT, IN THIS LOW-KEY, VERY CLUBBY ATMOSPHERE, PROTECTED BY A WALL OF SHRUBBERY from the traffic of boulevards Montparnasse and l'Observatoire, that the place got its name from a working-class ball? And of rather ill repute, to boot. The first Closerie opened across the street from it, and like the famous Grande Chaumière, attracted pimps as well as students who seemed to enjoy close calls with the police. On the corner where, for more than a century, "our" Closerie has been, there used to be an old canteen for coach drivers.

Time passes…but not so quickly at La Closerie. Since it opened its doors in its present incarnation, the establishment has always been a refuge for writers: Baudelaire, Verlaine, then Paul Fort (whose regular "Tuesdays" gathered together all of Parisian letters—Gide, Jarry, Carco…).

You can still make out familiar faces by the dimly lit mahogany bar: Once upon a time, Parisian singer Renaud, in his "Mister Renard" period, let the Ricard flow, as he sat alone in a corner surveying the room like a lighthouse guard. (The singer, known for his typical Parisian accent and attitude, went through a long period of oblivion during which he used to over-indulge at La Closerie. He called his inebriated alter ego "Renard."). Would he one day see his own name engraved in the table like other illustrious customers? Beckett, Man Ray, Sartre…

A grilled bass at the restaurant to the right, with a nice Sancerre and charming companion, remains a satisfyingly intimate experience, highly recommended for budding romances. But like all true lovers of La Closerie, we reserve our most ardent tenderness for the brasserie wing, for "the boat" with its fleshy red leather, its cozy mahogany, and the magical light that bathes couples in light and shadow. It isn't surprising that Hemingway wrote *The Sun Also Rises* here. In his bohemian days, the comfortable booth of La Closerie, where he sipped small *café-crèmes* and scribbled

in big blue notebooks, offered safe harbor between storms and stress— provided a meeting place, too, with Gertrude Stein or Dos Passos.

It still offers one a respite, a break from the bustle of Montparnasse. The veal liver is as oft-recommended as it is famous, but the poached haddock is a must, as maritime and as British as the decor. It seems the chef, formerly of Café Edgar, has a visible predilection for fish.

Le Montparnasse 1900

59, BOULEVARD DU MONTPARNASSE, 6TH ARR.

☎ 01 45 49 19 00   🚋 MONTPARNASSE-BIENVENUE

OPEN DAILY FROM NOON UNTIL MIDNIGHT

To TAKE A VOYAGE THROUGH THE SPACE-TIME CONTINUUM, ALL YOU HAVE TO DO IS TURN YOUR HEAD. FIRST TAKE THE boulevard Montparnasse exit from the Métro, walk a few steps to the west, and stop in the vestibule of Le Montparnasse 1900. Turn your head to the right, and there you are: in 1900, in this long gallery of mahogany-framed mirrors lined up on walls of polished ceramic Japonica tiles. Art Nouveau in all its splendor.

Turn your head to the left, and behold today's Montparnasse, and the tower that dominates the view with its mass of metal and glass. Esplanades

and promenades, slackers and office slaves carried along by the crowd; large expanses, chain restaurants, cineplexes.

The cozy ambiance of the Montparnasse 1900 is like a refuge from the ravages of time. It's no surprise that several tables are always taken up by dignified elderly ladies, seated alone in front of beautiful white tablecloths, a napkin slipped over the blouse, savoring the *plat du jour* along with a diminutive bottle of rosé. They come for the attentive service, and perhaps, a feeling that the frenetic pace of our present era can be, for a moment, slowed.

The establishment itself did not emerge untouched from the currents of the twentieth century. Opened by the Chartier brothers in 1901 on the site of an oyster merchant, it quickly became one of the jewels in their collection of *bouillons*, decorated by Louis Trézel, a disciple of Mucha who also worked on Julien. When the *bouillon* fell out  of favor, the Chartiers' great rival Rougeot, manager of Vagenende, took over. It prospered under the moniker Restaurant Rougeot until the war, then became Le Bistrot de la Gare, turning Michel Oliver into a household name. Restored by Slavik, it hung onto a perilous existence until Gérard Joulie finally added it to his collection, withholding this little gem from the coveting grasps of Flo and the family Blanc.

What to expect from such a timeless place if not an equally timeless cuisine? Why not choose the ultimate in simplicity: *rognon de veau entier*, served with a light mustard sauce and a red Sancerre.

Le Petit Lutétia

107, RUE DE SEVRES, 6TH ARR.

☎ 01 45 48 33 53   🚇 VANEAU, DUROC

OPEN DAILY FROM 11:30AM UNTIL 3:00PM

AND FROM 7:00PM UNTIL 11:00PM

NINETY YEARS OLD AND NOT A SINGLE WRINKLE! LE PETIT LUTÉTIA IS ALL THE HAPPIER THAT SHE HASN'T CHANGED a hair. It's true that the establishment, which was built at the same time as the building on the rue de Sevres that shelters it, was renovated some fifteen years ago by the present owner, Daniel Dahdah, but only to restore the classic floor mosaics and floral glass partitions to their original condition, to reinforce the velvet, and to return a bit of luster to the flowery ornaments on the chestnut-brown ceiling.

In this pleasant canteen, straight out of the Roaring Twenties, a handful of celebrities—Olivier Poivre d'Arvor and Régis Laspalès, last time we were there—discreetly indulge in the familiar and deceptively simple cuisine concocted by the chef, Robert Poignant.

The staff has the professional bearing of another era—attentive without being interfering—and seems to have been there forever. No small thing, mind you!

And the regulars who gather in the vestibule with an air of the bon vivant about them suggest that for many, Le Petit Lutétia is a lasting passion.

Don't look for adventure in the menu or on the metal easel brought to the table by the maître d' to advertise the specials of the day: everything is tried-and-true, mastered to perfection. The *bourguignon*, *cuissot de sanglier* or *confit*, but also *dorade*—all strike the perfect medium between richness and flavor.

This is a brasserie that exists outside of time, a space made to a human scale, a bit provincial, far from the affectations of the germanopratines. As for its name, the restaurant has always had it—long before the neighboring *"grand"* hotel opened its doors.

Le Petit Zinc

L E PETIT ZINC, OR HOW TO MAKE THE OLD NEW. AND VICE VERSA. BEGIN WITH A LOCKSMITH'S SHOP WITH A BEAUTIFUL Art Nouveau facade, with its ruby color and naive faience, created on the confines of the Saint Benedictine abbey. Add a bistro on the corner of the rue Guillaume Apollinaire. And down the street at the rue de Buci, a neighborhood institution, Le Petit Zinc. Let life, time, and business do their thing. The locksmith has become a retro restaurant, L'Assiette

au Beurre. Then Le Petit Zinc, under the management of the Layrac family, grows out of its cramped space and swallows up L'Assiette. The Blanc brothers come through with their enormous appetite and add the corner bistro to the mix, to create the brasserie we know now.

The Blanc brothers opened their new jewel box in 2000; their mixture of the authentic (the Guimard-inflected spirals of the facade, the traditional occupations depicted in the faience) and the chic (pretty, plump chairs with cutout backrests; multiple levels; an ambiance borrowed from 1930s Hollywood) continues to delight the tourists who come in after their *apéro* at the Deux Magots or Bonaparte. From the speakers, Sinatra tantalizes the ears of timid English couples with  his hopeless love for Ava Gardner, while a Spanish family decides to indulge in the *foie gras* and a table full of businessmen loosen their ties.

The fashionable wait staff waltz from table to table purveying the faultless cuisine that has made the Blancs' reputation—*banc de fruits de mer*, calf's liver, shoulder of lamb, the catch of the day—along with a perfectly serviceable petit Chablis from a wine list that is, it must be said, rather abbreviated.

Come summer, the opening of the terrace brings a surplus of kitschy languor to this corner of Saint-Germain-des-Prés, and with it a healthy dose of romantic nostalgia.

Le Procope

13, RUE DE L'ANCIENNE-COMEDIE, 6TH ARR.

☎ 01 40 46 79 00   🚇 ODEON

OPEN DAILY FROM NOON UNTIL MIDNIGHT

LET US RETURN TO CAESAR WHAT IS SO OFTEN WRONGLY ATTRIBUTED TO FRANCESCO. THE FIRST CAFÉ IN FRANCE opened its doors in Marseille in 1654. Le Procope, history's first Parisian café, came along only thirty-two years later. But let us also concede that all trace of this pioneering Marseillan has been lost—no doubt his account was quickly settled—whereas Le Procope lives on, after some 320 years of good and loyal service.

Now, think about this: a café is an establishment where the beverage after which it is named can be consumed. So, what is Le Procope: a café? An ice-cream shop? A restaurant? A brasserie? Perhaps it doesn't matter. In more than three centuries, the establishment founded in 1686 by an

Italian named Francesco Procopio dei Coltelli has had plenty of time
to challenge labels, and styles mix and mingle here as much as people
do. It owes its success and its longevity to the two menu items to which
it owes its reputation: the coffee, first of all, without which drinking
establishments in France might still be limited to rowdy taverns. And

the ice-cream dishes—sorbets and *mystères*—served for the first time at Le Procope, beneath its mirrors (another first for the era, which soon became the essential accessory to any restaurant's decor).

There is nothing that hasn't been said of Le Procope. The list of prestigious regulars would hardly fit within the tomes of the Encyclopedia of D'Alembert and Diderot—who, reportedly spent far less time here than the real pillar of the establishment, Voltaire. Verlaine suffered through his spleen here, surrounded by the timeless wainscoting. Revolutionaries Danton, Marat, and Robespierre conspired here so frequently and so well that management installed *fleur-de-lis* friezes on the first floor—they are still there for the viewing—in a kind of paradoxical homage.

Le Procope's renown owes much to its one-time neighbor, the Comedie-Française, which used to be located right across the street. Le Procope thus bore witness to all the most resounding successes and flops of the seventeenth and eighteenth centuries.

Like everything else, Le Procope became bourgeois, and hosted years upon years of Academicians' banquets and debates. Now it serves as a salon for the academy of coffee connoisseurs.

Amidst the many things that Le Procope introduced to French cuisine, one is often forgotten—the café waiter, or *garçon de café*. Georges Viaud, the expert on the matter, once expressed astonishment that these robust men of a certain age would be saddled with such a moniker. Until he discovered that the waiters at Le Procope in the *grand age* were, in fact, very young. What do the present-day "*garçons*"—and *filles*—of Le Procope serve? Classic brasserie food, which, though hardly adventurous, keeps alive the patina of the place, its history, and its ambiance.

Le Select

99, RUE DU MONTPARNASSE, 6TH ARR.

☎ 01 45 48 38 24 / 01 42 22 65 27

🚇 VAVIN, MONTPARNASSE-BIENVENUE

OPEN DAILY FROM 7:00AM UNTIL 2:30AM;

3:30AM ON FRIDAY AND SATURDAY

THIS IS A GOOD PLACE TO BECOME KNOWN BY YOUR FIRST NAME. PHILIPPE, THE BARTENDER WITH THE IMPECCABLY fitted green jacket, has been fielding the confidences and soccer tales of regulars, both famous and anonymous, for thirty years. Ernest? He sat right there, Philippe tells you, gesturing to a corner of the bar, his movements as composed and precise as they'll be when he describes last night's winning goal. And he could just as easily have mentioned Pablo, Scott, Michel, Philippe, Romane, Vincent—without your ever being sure that he is actually referring to the people you imagine.

The boss, though, is Francis. Monsieur Francis. It's thanks to him that Le Select became a brasserie at all. Tired of disappointing customers who would ask about food after inhaling the fragrances of staff meals, he finally made the leap in 1990. A brasserie it is.

Francis is the benevolent master of his world, his little corner of Montparnasse: the terrace, where the almost-famous sit side by side with weekend lovers and tourists in search of lost time, all gazing contemplatively out onto the boulevard; the dining room whose wooden tables are as old as the restaurant; the mirrors that have reflected the traits of so

Huitres Spéciales N°4
" GILLARDEAU "
les 6 = 14€ les 9 = 20€50 les 12 = 27€

SOLE MEUNIÈRE   €24,20

CÔTE BOEUF (2 Per.) €55,60
PAVE CHEVILLARD   €24,50

★ Farfalles gratinées au Cantal 9€
★ Hachis de poissons S.Verte 14€60
★ Entrecôte grillée Beurre
                maître d'Hôtel 1480
Tartelette aux noix 7€

DRIX NETS

75

many familiar faces; the backroom where Pierre (Assouline) held court. If you want to brighten Philippe's day, talk to him of the color green—

not the green of his restaurant's insignia, but of the popular soccer club,
the Verts of Saint-Étienne. Yes, life in this place moves to the capricious

rhythms of a round ball.

When they opened the first all-night café in Paris, in 1924, the Jalberts must have expected to see some strange birds fly in. They gave it a name from across the Atlantic—for an American flavor—and lo and behold, every Yankee in Paris soon wound up here, belly to the bar. Where else could they go? Everything was closed. Hemingway, Dos Passos, Fitzgerald, Miller—all would regularly make this their last stop (after a night at La Closerie, La Rotonde, or La Coupole).

It is said that the Jalberts looked on them with suspicious eyes, and they had even less affection for the entourage of Kiki of Montparnasse, who adopted the terrace as her hunting ground. But it was the wildlife of Montparnasse that would make Le Select an institution—unchangeable in a way, and yet altered whenever it changed hands, from the Jalberts to Plegat, father and son. And now, Francis.

As the latter emphasizes, the difficulty for a café that is, after all, selective, is "to make improvements without changing anything." Case in point: the expansion to restaurant service, now responsible for 70% of Le Select's business. Francis offers a traditional menu—no bells and whistles, just flawless taste—like Le Select.

Francis, Philippe, Ernie, and the rest—forget them. The real star of the Select is the one whose portrait looms over the left side of the bar: Mickey. With a mustache to compete with the best of them, a color as deep and shimmering as the best red wine (though with a bit of a tiger stripe)—the resident cat has become the mascot of all Montparnasse.

And a first name is all he's ever had.

Vagenende

142, BOULEVARD SAINT-GERMAIN, 6TH ARR.

☎ 01 43 26 68 18 🚋 ODÉON, MABILON

OPEN DAILY FROM NOON UNTIL MIDNIGHT

VAGENENDE (PRONOUNCED VAJEUNANDE) DECLARES ITS STRONG SUIT RIGHT OFF: ITS SIGN PROCLAIMS — IN SIZABLE letters—"restaurant." The word "brasserie" only appears, much smaller, on the window blinds. It's true that, compared to Paris' giant factories of fine cuisine, Vagenende is a small brasserie. It also takes intimacy seriously—maybe because it is run by a woman—and provides shelter for its customers in the form of mini-alcoves, set up against the bronze pillars that have supported the roof (as well as countless coats that have been hung upon their hooks) since 1878.

But make no mistake. The ambiance is Parisian in the extreme. Even the player piano (fabricated in Roubaix), which holds court to the right of the entryway atop a handsome sideboard, makes that abundantly clear, churning out "Un Gamin de Paris" to the delight of a group of Japanese tourists. This place doesn't have the sheer enormity of Chartier, or the imposing brightness of Julien; you'll hear more whispers here than guffaws. And yet it began, in 1904—after a brief incarnation as a *pâtisserie*—as a real *bouillon*, run by the Chartier brothers and designed with the same care they bestowed on all their projects.

Beveled mirrors eye each other from one end of the room to the other, much like they do in Le Montparnasse 1900—a kissing cousin of Vagenende, both historically and architecturally. But the real showstopper at Vagenende has to be the thirty-six landscapes on *pâte-de-verre* by painter Guillaume Pivain, which provide context to the fruit-themed embellishments of the walls' faience. In effect, the glass pieces serve to protect this former inner courtyard from both inclement weather and the damaging rays of the sun.

Kissing cousins, with some rivalry: the erstwhile owner of the Montparnasse 1900, Rougeot, bought the business from the Chartiers in 1923 when their *bouillon* enterprise was crumbling. Rougeot then relinquished it to the Vagenende family, which kept it running for half a century.

Like so many of Paris' best and most beautiful institutions, Vagenende nearly lost all its ornate glory to the renovating spirit of the 1960s: if not for the intervention of Andre Malraux himself, the Vagenende would be a supermarket today (and tomorrow, a drugstore?).

The menu—*pot-au-feu, pied de cochon, cassoulet, coq au vin*—is proof that when it comes to cuisine, Vagenende relies on its most irreplaceable patron saint: the land.

Chez Françoise

AÉROGARE DES INVALIDES, 7TH ARR.

☎ 01 47 05 49 03 🚇 INVALIDES

OPEN DAILY FROM NOON UNTIL MIDNIGHT

YES, YOU COULD BEMOAN THE FACT THAT PASCAL MOUSSET WOULD SACRIFICE THE NEOCOLONIAL DÉCOR THAT, SINCE the 1950s, had given Chez Françoise its mildly exotic charm. But this rising star of culinary Paris wanted to make a statement, and there is nothing to reproach in the new club-style ambiance, which is augmented in the evenings with a touch of jazz.

Fortunately, the new team in charge of this fine institution—improbably located under the airport bus terminal at Les Invalides—has kept a key item on the menu: the *crêpe Suzette de Monsieur Ali*, named for the waiter who used to perform the dessert's flaming preparation with the dexterity of a flying ace.

The aviation metaphor is appropriate: Chez Françoise is the unexpected brainchild of Air France, which in 1949 decided to open a prestigious restaurant on the premises (which it owns)—a strange paradox, this sort of subterranean jumbo jet.

The locale made Françoise a real oddity, with its viewless terrace tucked snugly away beneath the vast esplanade of Les Invalides. Françoise was the nickname given to the manageress, who, along with the proprietor of the restaurant Chez Rousseau, was the first to service this cabin in 1949. In the heady early years of the pioneering Caravelle jetliner, passengers would wait at a table for their flight to be announced; those departing would make their way to the Orly airport, and later to Roissy. Members of Parliament came, too, remembering the meals served up by Rousseau when he was in charge of the kitchen at the Assemblée Nationale. They remained faithful, inspiring the *menu parliamentaire* which Pascal Mousset, out of respect for universal suffrage, has retained on the menu. In its second youth, Françoise now infuses its dishes with the exoticism once reserved for its woodwork: *Foie gras* and *sole meunière* uphold tradition, but the rocket and peppers, the cilantro and parmesan betray a South-facing wanderlust.

Thoumieux

79, RUE SAINT-DOMINIQUE, 7TH ARR.

☎ 01 47 05 49 75 🚇 INVALIDES

OPEN MONDAY THROUGH SUNDAY FROM NOON UNTIL MIDNIGHT

THIS IS JIM HARRISON AT THOUMIEUX: "I ORDERED GRILLED SARDINES, SOME ESCARGOTS, *FOIE GRAS*, ROASTED GUINEA hen, *cassoulet*, and a rib steak. The waiter, who knew me, was mildly shocked, but then I explained to him that I was going back to the Great North, far away from any French food. He muttered, his voice filled with pity, 'Poor poet.'"

Those who know how much the American novelist likes to lift his fork (not to mention his glass) won't be surprised to learn that he considers this, quite simply, "the best restaurant in Paris." He is joined by other outspoken writers—Eric Neuhoff, Patrick Besson, Thierry Ardisson—who, probably lured by Denis Tillinac (he's as at home here as in Corrèze), have all done their time playing New World conquerors at Thoumieux. A Legend of the Fall (and of the bistro) claims that a president once dined with his daughter at table seventeen.

Harrison got the (very large) escargots. The Corrézians would easily go for the *tête de veau*, or for a good piece of *faux-filet limousine*. For the conquerors? *Cassoulet*, or else *éscalope de foie gras pôelée*. Mistakes are rare in the only brasserie in Paris to have a staff butcher, Christian Groner. Freshness is guaranteed.

The ornate carved-wood chairs have supported the weight of ministers; the red-velvet benches welcome "the people"; the white tablecloths have been graced by many a poet's elbow; and the old glass globes have amplified the outbursts of at least one rugby player. But it's all just part of the game; time goes on and things take their course, quietly, without the place changing in tempo or philosophy. The staff—charming waitresses, dashing maitre d', young and spirited doorman—welcomes entering customers with an almost conspiratorial warmth. Thoumieux is a family affair, and you are family as soon as you cross the threshold.

All in all, quite a success story for its forbear, Martial Thoumieux, all the way from Saint-Julien-le-Vendomois! A photo of him, along with one of his wife, hangs above the cash register, next to the cupboard for the hotel room keys. When the Thoumieuxs arrived in Paris, in the first decade of the twentieth century, they had it pretty tough. He was a dishwasher, and she worked as a waitress. In 1911, they bought a *bar-tabac*. In 1923, Thoumieux opened its doors. Their son, Roger, cut his teeth at the Café de la Paix. He took the reins of the family business in 1950. A quarter-century later, his son-in-law, Jean Bassalert, took over, developing the business without ever betraying its spirit. Now, a Thoumieux has appeared in Brussels, at the hands of a nephew; and a Café Thoumieux serves the thirsty just a few doors down from the original restaurant. Once a family, always a family...François Bassalert, the most recent and robust leader of the new line, represents the fourth generation.

Here, even the meat is part of the family; the cows—Christian Groner prefers the taste of the females—boast the appellation, "born to known parents."

L'Alsace

39, AVENUE DES CHAMPS-ELYSÉES, 8TH ARR.

☎ 01 53 93 97 00   🚇 FRANKLIN-D-ROOSEVELT

OPEN DAILY 24 HOURS

WHILE THE BLANC BROTHERS PROFOUNDLY REINVENTED THEIR BRASSERIE ON THE PLACE DES TERNES, LA LORRAINE, they barely touched this institution of the Champs-Elysées, always a focal point on the corner of the rue Marbeuf—twenty-four hours a day, seven days a week.

All that L'Alsace has to offer can be found right here on the Champs: the terrace facing the mythical avenue graciously welcomes tourists, who happily feast on the postcard view of Paris. The sauerkraut is first-class—as is the bill: location has its cost!

The room's inlaid woodwork and walls of mirrors are brightly lit both day and night, a continuous advertisement for this Alsatian brasserie. But it's only after midnight that the true charms of the place are revealed. Night owls and revelers, arriving in the darkest hours of night, cluster together like a ballet of mosquitoes around a lamp. This is where Jacques Blanc cut his teeth, back in 1982, continuing the nocturnal tradition the family started with Au Pied de Cochon. On Saturday nights the dining room never empties; people's expressions become vaguer, their conversations more rambling, as the hours pass. There's nothing like a plate of sauerkraut or a seafood platter to bring the life back to an exhausted party-hopper or a drowsing couple.

When the first tentative rays of dawn graze the mirrors and tables to compete with the light of the chandeliers, a languor softly descends. A champagne breakfast on the terrace is a rare pleasure—at an hour when the fear of cliché loses its grip, you may find yourself humming, "It's five o'clock; Paris awakes…" as you watch the street-cleaners slowly trundle up the avenue. L'Alsace never sleeps.

Le Boeuf sur le Toit

34, RUE DU COLISÉE, 8TH ARR.

☎ 01 53 93 65 55   🚇 SAINT-PHILLIPE-DU-ROULE

OPEN DAILY FROM NOON UNTIL MIDNIGHT

MORE THAN ONE BRASSERIE IN THIS GUIDE CAN CLAIM TO HAVE FREQUENTLY PLAYED HOST TO THE ARTISTS AND writers of bohemian Paris. It should come as no surprise, given its name (which means "the steer on the roof"), that Le Boeuf sur le Toit was, hands down, the culinary temple of Dadaism—and since then of a Paris that is no longer labeled trendy (though that doesn't mean it isn't).

With Jean Cocteau as its master drinker, the literary avant-garde of early-twentieth-century Paris ate, sang, painted, rhymed, and reveled in this place with the incongruous name. It was taken from the title of a pantomime co-authored by Cocteau and Darius Milhaud, and based on a Brazilian lament. Cocteau mentioned it to the proprietor, Louis Mayses, when he was still at Gaya, the small bar where Cocteau was a regular. The *enfant terrible* of French letters tells it like this: "Mayses begged me to let him have the name for his bar — as if it would bring him luck. That's the whole explanation behind the sign that some people have found so shocking, but that is not in fact any stranger than the Cheval Vert or Au Chien qui Fume. But its luck *has* been extremely good. It became a meeting place for artists, editors, and theater directors."

And what does it matter if this beef has changed roofs several times? When it opened, in 1922, at 28, rue Boissy-d'Anglas (near the Madeleine), the Boeuf attracted the artistic elite of Paris: Picasso, Man Ray, Tristan Tzara, Fernand Léger, and Francis Picabia, whose *L'Oeil cacodylate* graced the restaurant's walls. But there were also Maurice Chevalier, Mistinguett, André Gide...

At the piano, Jean Wiener raised the roof along with his friend Clément Doucet, making up rhymes for the good of the cause: jazz with Boissy d'Anglazz. Cocteau was there, of course, and Radiguet by his side: "In a subdued setting that contrasted with the violent colors that were in fashion, everyone crowded together: artists and those who came to see them; famous women who spent their days as far apart from each other as stars, but at night sparkled side by side against the beige and black sky."

The success of the establishment inspired it to spread its wings. The *"esprit boeuf"* became a wandering spirit, changing addresses five times before 1941. The animal wound up grazing the Elysian fields of the Champs, finally — or right next to it, on this quiet corner of the rue du Colisée.

Given a face-lift in 2002, it lost none of its charm, its woodwork, or its mirrors. Within its five discrete rooms, anyone who counts in Paris — a city more realist than surrealist these days — will eventually turn up.

La Fermette Marbeuf

5, RUE MARBEUF, 8TH ARR.

☎ 01 53 23 08 00   🚇 ALMA-MARCEAU, FRANKLIN-D-ROOSEVELT

OPEN DAILY FROM NOON UNTIL 11:30PM

THE DECOR OF LA FERMETTE MARBEUF IS SOMETHING TO RAVE ABOUT MORE THAN A CENTURY AFTER ITS CREATION. A miracle, when you think about all the sumptuous restaurants and cafés—daily bread for an Alphonse Allais at the turn of the last century—that haven't survived, that have been erased, massacred by the insatiable appetite for instant gratification.

It was a lucky stroke of a pick-axe—during a scheduled demolition in 1978—that unearthed the beauty of the original structure. Beneath the disbelieving eyes of the workers, a sublime interior of Art Nouveau ceramic and delicately ornate leaded glass bearing peacocks and sunflowers appeared, all in what had been used as a stockroom for a soulless restaurant. Four years later, rumor has it, an art collector demanded to see the circa-1900 room: he rec-

ognized the decor of a winter garden he'd seen at an auction in Maisons-Laffitte. The separated twins were reunited at the cost of exacting work: each facet of the windows, created in 1898 by Hubert and Martineau, was dismantled and reassembled on site, giving this jewel of the Blanc group its current luster.

At the close of the nineteenth century, it was the dining room of the Hôtel Langham on the rue du Boccador, which had been decorated by a young architect by the name of Émile Hurte and the ceramist Jules Wielhorski. It's a quiet masterpiece that had failed to resist the cruelty of two wars, not to mention the shifts in fashion. The Blanc brothers were right to preserve this setting, in which celebrities find refuge in a windowed marvel as magnificent, if not as recognized, as those of Bofinger.

The menu, as delicate as the structure, is slowly building its own set of classics: *feuilleté aux escargots*, garlic butter soufflé, saddle of lamb with a choron sauce, veal chops cooked traditionally or in a fondant of bitter chocolate.

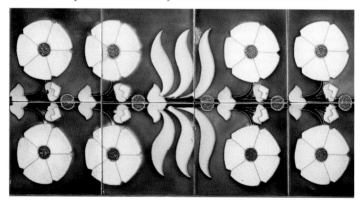

Fouquet's

99, AVENUE DES CHAMPS-ELYSÉES, 8TH ARR.

☎ 01 47 23 70 60   🚇 GEORGES-V

OPEN DAILY FROM 7:30AM UNTIL MIDNIGHT

ESTABLISHED IN 1899 AT "99, THE MOST BEAUTIFUL AVENUE IN THE WORLD," FOUQUET'S HAS MANAGED TO BECOME the unrivaled canteen, bistro, and second home to the Parisian film world and other jet setters of the city. And, now, a bar-hotel: Lucien Barriere's company, which has bought up the business, is in the process of transforming the building next door to Paris' most famous brasserie into a palace on the scale of the Champs Elysées; it will have one hundred suites.

When Louis Fouquet bought it, this was a small coachman's bar called Le Criterion, and the jet set didn't exist. But English was already in vogue,

which explains the anglophone apostrophe in the name—like a wink from the sign, tempting the most privileged tourists to come in and be seen on the most visible terrace in Paris. It was Fouquet's successor, Léopold Mourier, who made the place a palace of pleasure for rich merchants but also for the spirited pilots who took to the skies on the eve of the First

World War. And that's how the very exclusive barroom came to be called the "squadron's bar," in honor of French aviation.

Between the wars, Fouquet's reputation grew, and anyone who was anyone in Paris—from actors (Gabin) to gangsters (Carbone), from directors (Carné) to gamblers (Marcel Francisci), from successful authors (Guitry, Pagnol) to successful businessmen—showed up there. Then José Artur, a fixture at Fouquet's—so much so that the new chef, Jean-Yves Leuranguer, named a dish after him—set his ubiquitous radio program, *Pop Club*, here. In 1976, Maurice Casanova took over the mythical place, and, along with his accomplice, Georges Cravenne, has hosted the César (the French Oscars), the Molière, and several literary awards ceremonies here.

When it turned a century old and was acquired by the Lucien Barrière enterprise in 1999, Fouquet's, always in keeping with the times, charged

Jacques Garcia—THE decorator for all who dine and sleep in Paris—with the task of breathing new life into it; just nine years earlier it had been added to the directory of landmark buildings.

Between studied stylishness and respect for tradition, chef Jean-Yves Leuranguer has refashioned Fouquet's menu to offer a light and mildly adventurous cuisine. The future would look good, if not for the fact that a former merchant, Lina Renault, has laid claim to the property, in the name of an ancestor from whom she alleges it was wrongfully usurped. For the moment, the Société des restaurants du Café de Paris, owner of the building, has been awarded just cause by the courts, but Lina Renault won't lay down her arms (she won in the latest court decision but an appeal has been lodged). For in France, unlike in other countries in Europe, the right to property doesn't expire at the end of ninety-nine years.

La Lorraine

2, PLACE DES TERNES, 8TH ARR.

☎ 01 56 21 22 00   🚇 TERNES

OPEN DAILY FROM 7:00AM UNTIL 1:00AM

ANY ESTABLISHMENT THAT OCCUPIES ALMOST A QUARTER OF THE TOTAL SIDEWALK AREA OF THE PLACE DES TERNES becomes a part of the city's landscape. So it was an altogether risky move at the end of 2004 to change everything, to redo everything, to completely re-think the appearance of this neighborhood monument, this venerable bastion of the Art Deco brasserie tradition.

Regular customers, older patrons, even the staff sometimes wonder, still, whether the bright, austere course adopted by the architect Jean-Pierre Heim was the right one to take, flouting as it did the traditional canon of the brasserie. But after you let the blond marble exert its charms, revel in the disparate ambiances afforded by each space, and linger upon the frescoes that were exhumed during the renovations (look under your feet as you walk in), you will be won over by the renewed spirit of one of the Blanc brothers' most winning establishments. The architect, who is better known for his work in New York, wanted to imbue the place with a transatlantic ambiance. And so it is that the breeze of the high sea seems to sweep across the deck of this terrace, located to the starboard of a rather stern square.

So much business has blown in on this new wind that La Lorraine is out of breath. Its more international—less Parisian—look has proved

inviting to the British and Japanese tourists, who sit down to sumptuous seafood platters and line-caught bass of the highest order.

The waiters are as cosmopolitan as an ad for a certain Italian sweater company, as varied in origin as they are uniform in attire: the classic garb of a *garçon de café* with the addition of whimsical neckties. The service remains Parisian—just deferent enough, attentive but not aggressively so—but English, German, Italian, and even Chinese are spoken here. The staff is prepared for anything, and nothing trips them up; if you stand next to the second column to the right of the door, you can watch the intricate dance of servers entering and exiting the kitchen—plenty of near-misses, never a collision.

On the menu? Products of the high seas, and a delightful wine list filled with Bordeaux and Burgundies. It's the little marks of attention, the almost imperceptible touches, that make all the difference. A light consommé to start, a meringue served with the coffee, olive oil in a pretty dish to accompany the fish, an assortment of mustards (with grated horseradish) arrayed next to a perfectly cooked *foie de veau*.

While you may see fewer famous faces at La Lorraine than in its heyday in the 1930s, this *paquebot* has definitely found its cruising speed.

Mollard

115, RUE SAINT-LAZARE, 8TH ARR.

☎ 01 43 87 50 22   🚇 SAINT-LAZARE

OPEN DAILY FROM NOON UNTIL 12:30AM

HERE IS A PRIME ILLUSTRATION OF THE CLASSIC STORY OF THE GREAT BRASSERIE: GLORY, DECLINE...AND RENAISSANCE. The Mollards came from their native Savoie in 1867 to settle in this area of Paris—at the time a space somewhere between city and countryside—where the Gare Saint-Lazare had just opened up for service. They bought a small café, Le Bougnat, and day by day, as the train station brought more and more travelers to the neighborhood, their fortune grew—one glass of beer, wine, or absinthe at a time.

And so Monsieur Mollard began to think bigger. At the turn of the century, the trend was running toward brasseries. They were to that decade what drugstores were to the 1960s, Philippe Starck-style cafés to the 1980s, and fast-food joints to the 1990s. Mollard built the most grandiose, the most "brasserie" of all brasseries. He spared no expense, enlisting Edouard Niermans, the most sought-after architect of the moment, who had built the

Negresco at Nice, the Hotel de Paris in Monte Carlo, the Angelina tea salon and the Moulin-Rouge. The opening, on September 14, 1895, was attended by anyone who was anyone in Paris.

Italian ceramic, marble columns prefiguring Art Deco, vast mirrors, rampant Orientalism, Mucha-influenced murals, a Japanese accent. The Mollard feels a little like a very deluxe bathhouse, and thanks to the subtle play of mirrors, its sumptuous decor seems to go on forever.

Art Nouveau was begun. It would not survive the First World War—and neither would the fortunes of the Mollards. The establishment passed into the hands of the Gauthier family, and the opulent decor disappeared beneath the coats of paint that were the order of the day.

Business wouldn't pick up until the housing crisis of the 1950s. Businessmen fresh off the train from Normandy would come to Mollard to sign contracts over their aperitifs before heading back home; they used the brasserie as their office. In the 1960s, it was the *"omelette-surprise"*—a catchall dish sold for the bargain price of ten francs—that kept the Mollard in the black.

Everyone—or nearly everyone—had forgotten about the erstwhile glamour of the place, until the day in 1965 when the decision was made to look behind the mirrors and beneath the layers of white paint for the original decor. And memories of the Belle Epoque came flooding back.

More than a century after its opening, this stunning location continues to delight a diverse clientele—travelers, professionals from the neighborhood, old regulars. Perhaps the best seat in the house is in the small pink salon to the right of the entryway, where the whole team of Mollard—Albert, the intellectual; Jean-Claude, the old-timer; José, the joker; Marc, the man of the evening—hustle without interruption behind a colossal sideboard placed in view of the diners. They aren't kidding around. And, with a little bit of luck, you'll also meet Huguette, the faithful regular who is so at home in her surroundings that American tourists sometimes call her "Madame Mollard."

Le Café de la Paix

2, RUE SCRIBE, 9TH ARR.

☎ 01 40 07 36 36   🚇 OPÉRA

OPEN DAILY FROM 7:00AM UNTIL 11:30PM

WITHOUT A DOUBT, THIS IS THE MOST WELL-KNOWN CAFÉ IN PARIS. AND THE MOST EXPENSIVE, TOO. BUT THERE has to be one, so why not this one, which shares its name with the most valuable property in French Monopoly (their version of Boardwalk)? Arriving in Paris, Hemingway faced the unwelcome surprise of discovering the cost of life in the capital city: in 1921, the writer invited his wife Hadley to dinner here but couldn't afford to pay the rather lofty bill. The American had come to look for traces of former regulars Proust and Maupassant in the opulent walls. It would be impossible to count the number of distinguished guests who have gathered around the marble pedestal tables, or rested their illustrious feet upon the bronze lion-paws on the café table bases. But the most famous, and the most emblematic,

would surely be General de Gaulle, who had his first meal after Paris' liberation here, in this café so perfectly named for the event. (History did not make a note of whether or not he paid his bill.)

While politicians—this was the bastion of Bonapartistes during the Second Empire—have always been

patrons of this oversized dining room of the adjacent Grand Hotel, writers came along later, after the composers and singers from the neighboring Opéra (which shared a designer—Charles Garnier—with the café). Massenet or Verdi would dine here after a triumph. Masked balls, very popular with *haute société*—were also held here.

When the place de l'Opéra was settled, between 1862 and 1864, its developers opted for a balance of ostentation and good taste. An unwritten rule requires the conservation of that standing, and the 2003 renovation of the Café de la Paix scrupulously respected the spirit of its locale.

The proximity of deluxe shopping and its central spot on every guidebook tour of "Paris by Night" have made Café de la Paix a beacon for tourists. But then, it's almost more monument than brasserie anyway. As one worldly chronicler put it as far back as 1882, "It is a marvelous palace which anyone in the world may enter."

Charlot, Roi des Coquillages

81, BOULEVARD DE CLICHY, 9TH ARR.

☎ 01 53 20 48 00   🚇 PLACE-DE-CLICHY

OPEN DAILY FROM NOON UNTIL MIDNIGHT

ACROSS FROM THE GRAND CINEMAS OF THE PLACE DE CLICHY, CHARLOT PROUDLY DISPLAYS ITS SWEET LITTLE face, straight out of a Hollywood movie of the 1930s. Art Deco to the extreme, this large seafood restaurant announces its noble claim without embarrassment: the king of shellfish. If this slightly kitschy monument, which teasingly faces the venerable Wepler, seems full of bluster, that might be its Marseillean side. Charlot is the only restaurant in Paris to have been armed by the signatories of the charter of the *bouillabaisse* (otherwise all natives of the Phocaean city or its environs). And it must be admitted that the *bouillabaisse* at Charlot is top-notch—the broth sufficiently subtle to allow the fish to fully express their flavors.

It should also be said that Charlot, one of the best of the Blanc brothers' offerings, is no factory: its two floors, laden with marine frescoes and tortoise shells, promise privacy in a temple to the products of a silent world. On the red-velvet seats, tourists and locals feast on perfectly balanced soup, delicate aïoli, or the Mediterranean grilled fish that can be found hardly anywhere else in this city, far from any ocean.

And, even as their eyes drift up to the mirrored ceilings, they concede without question that Charlot's title is well-deserved.

Chartier

7, RUE DU FAUBOURG-MONTMARTRE, 9TH ARR.

☎ 01 47 70 86 29   🚇 GRANDES-BOULEVARDS

OPEN DAILY FROM NOON UNTIL MIDNIGHT

HERE IS THE SOLE REMAINDER OF THE CHARTIER BROTH-ERS' PIONEERING SPIRIT. THE LAST *BOUILLON* THAT BEARS their name perpetuates a spirit, a soul, an idea that is very simple: to properly serve, without pretension and at a fair price, Parisians from seven to seventy-seven, from welfare recipients to those in the highest tax bracket.

For the tourist in search of remnants of Arletty's Paris, Chartier is no less necessary a stop than the flea market at Saint-Ouen, the place du Tertre, or a ride on the *bâteau-mouche*. Of course here, those partial to an intimate atmosphere, delicate flavors, deferential service, and a final bill folded in thirds and solemnly delivered, will be disappointed. This simply isn't their world. You don't sell Cartier watches at Tati. Chartier is a rare vestige of unpretentiousness, which delights anyone nostalgic for the canteen or the

university café: real devotees will still come here to eat an *oeuf mayo* some ten, twenty, thirty years after graduation.

This particular *bouillon* was run by Camille, the elder of the Chartier brothers, and almost nothing has changed since the day in 1896 when, picking up on the idea of the butcher Duval, the Chartiers began serving up their beef broth and vegetables to the Parisian worker.

It's hard to play the snob surrounded by this timeless decor, amidst such a convivial gathering of lone students, elderly people in search of company, tourists fleeing the high prices of the City of Light, and shoppers taking a rest between sessions. Yes, it's fast food—of course. And the service—so Spartan and expedient, the bill scrawled on the tablecloth with no regard for discretion—might offend some delicate souls. But there *are* servers; we aren't in a hamburger chain. And even if some of the most well-known fast-food chains occasionally invest in locations with historical import, none of those "restaurants" (if you can call them that) occupies a setting like this one—a registered landmark, with mirrors and stained glass, Art Nouveau flowers and *boiserie*. The decor is a distillation of the Chartier challenge: to serve the proletariat in a bourgeois setting. Chartier has served fifty million real meals at this single address! Since 1954, the Lemaire family has kept the flame—which, like the light from the chandeliers, flickers at around 3:30 to announce siesta time.

Le Grand Café

4, BOULEVARD DES CAPUCINES, 9TH ARR.

☎ 01 43 12 19 00   🚇 OPERA, RICHELIEU-DROUOT

OPEN DAILY 24 HOURS

AFTER THE PIED DE COCHON—ACQUIRED BY THEIR FATHER, CLÉMENT, IN 1946—LE GRAND CAFÉ DES CAPUCINES became the flagship of the Blanc brothers, the headquarters of their company, and its showpiece. How could it be otherwise?

Before them, two famous brothers departed in search of a new world. The Lumière brothers presented their invention for the first time in public, before thirty-three paying spectators (among them Georges Méliès), in the basement of the Grand Café. At the time it was at number 14, not in its current spot on the boulevard, and it backed up against the Paramount cinema, which in turn picked up the flame of the magic lantern in 1927. At number 6, there was another well-known nineteenth-century establishment: the Grande Maison Blanc. So it isn't hard to understand why, in 1977, Pierre Blanc took possession of the property, while his brother Jacques was acquiring La Taverne.

In this district of luxury and indulgence, just steps from the Opéra, the elder Blanc brother has created a familiar ambiance: like Au Pied de Cochon and L'Alsace, Le Grand Café never closes its doors. Seven days a week, twenty-four hours a day, the establishment invites tourists, music lovers, and night owls to return to its Art Nouveau decor and its classic brasserie cuisine—not a lot of risk,

but never a disappointment. Charles Trenet sang something to the effect of: "At the Grand Café, you enter randomly, dazzled by the lights from the boulevard."

Random choices can be the best ones, providing opportunities that might otherwise have been missed — like the chance to taste, for example, the twice-roasted duck with olives and turnips, or the warm Grand Marnier soufflé that is still the house dessert. Very recently, the menu has been expanded a bit and become a little more adventurous. So much the better.

At night, the feverish atmosphere on the main level will warm the heart; during the day, you may want to dine more privately on the second floor, beneath the beautiful stained-glass window.

La Taverne

24, BOULEVARD DES ITALIENS, 9TH ARR.

☎ 01 55 53 10 00   🚇 RICHELIEU-DROUOT

OPEN DAILY FROM NOON UNTIL MIDNIGHT,

FRIDAYS AND SATURDAYS UNTIL 1:00AM

ANOTHER BASTION OF THE BROTHERS BLANC, LA TAVERNE WAS THE ORIGINAL PROJECT OF THE ELDEST, JEAN-FRANÇOIS, who has since passed it on to his brothers. This unpretentious—and in many ways unextraordinary—brasserie on the corner of the boulevards Haussmann and des Italiens offers the ideal spot for a relaxing break, somewhere between Parisian cliché and international ambiance. The nineteenth-century-inspired decor, which is punctuated by period clocks on the walls and soft music in the background, is no doubt an homage to the history of the building.

At the turn of the century, it belonged to the marquise of Hertford—an Italian, despite the name—who leased the ground floor to the Café de Paris, a favorite haunt of Musset, Balzac, and Théophile Gautier. The café bestowed "*boulevardiers*" diplomas on its regulars, and the marquise had a single rule: that the establishment close at 10pm so that she could sleep in peace. La Taverne has freed itself from this constriction, now closing after midnight—one hour later even than the exception granted to another former regular, Lord Seymour, one of the most famously fun-loving nobles of his times. The menu of the old Café de Paris has been lost to memory; but at La Taverne, sauerkraut and seafood have pride of place.

Brasserie Flo

THIS IS WHERE JEAN-PAUL BUCHER LAID THE FIRST STONE OF HIS EMPIRE; IN THIS DARK COURTYARD, WEDGED IN between the Gare de l'Est and the boulevards, which once was home to the Sun King's stables, he wrote the first chapter of his legend. With due respect to Louis XIV, the sun is rarely seen in the cour des Petites-Écuries, but the play of shadows is part of Flo's charm. Perhaps the brasserie's only two owners—Bucher now, and before him Floderer, whose name

126

would be adopted by a future empire—saw a resemblance to the winter shadows of their native Alsace? "Well before I bought Flo, I was already in love with the place. Let's say I had a sense, a sentiment, a presentiment about its nature and its historic and cultural specificity," explains the current king of the realm.

Along with Bofinger, which Bucher would also buy up later, Floderer became one of the best manifestations of the fad for Alsatian brasseries that was set off by the Universal Expositions of 1857 and 1868, when Parisian visitors to the German pavilion discovered the pleasures of beer and sauerkraut. Floderer had initially named his establishment Chez Hans, which turned out to pose some problems; the brasserie was sacked during the Germanophobia of the War. So the boss gave it his own name in 1916—and an insignia that would make the fortune of an ambitious enterprise, half a century later. Floderer was strategically placed—just a few steps away from the Gare de l'Est, into which shipments of cold beer arrived each day. In a way, it also launched the catering service that Bucher would later fully develop—Sarah Bernhardt, who was starring at La Renaissance, would have him deliver meals prepared to her tastes. In May of 1968, Jean-Paul Bucher, won over by the particular atmosphere of the place—its bronze statuettes, bewitching mirrors, subtle marquetry— bought Flo. And the revolution began.

The rapid ascent of this humble cook from Molsheim, who came to Paris with only his degree from a technical school in his pocket, didn't please everyone—far from it. But, very quickly, he established his golden triangle in the tenth arrondisement, buying up Julien, a couple steps away, and then the Terminus Nord.

Today, Flo counts twenty-two brasseries in its stable, not counting its chains, Hippopotamus and Bistro Romain. But only this, the first one, benefits from that ineffable, soulful quality that we expect from the creation of a true pioneer.

Julien

16, RUE DU FAUBOURG-SAINT-DENIS, 10TH ARR.

☎ 01 47 70 12 06   🚇 STRASBOURG-SAINT-DENIS

OPEN DAILY FROM NOON UNTIL 1:00AM

THE RUE FAUBOURG-SAINT-DENIS HAS UNDERGONE A SERIOUS FACE-LIFT THESE PAST YEARS, LOSING A BIT OF its famous proletarian grit and uncovering the appeals of its wide flagstone sidewalks; but walking into Julien still produces a shock. Nestled between shacks selling kebabs, this small Art Nouveau treasure seems to be completely preserved from the passage of time.

The biggest-name designers of the 1880s and 1890s were hired by then-owner Édouard Fournier, and they made Julien a magical place. Louis Majorelle, the most famous cabinetmaker from the École de Nancy, is responsible for the bar made of Cuban ebony. A subtle light is diffused by a stained-glass window created by the Guenne workshop—and not, as is sometimes rumored, by Bernard Buffet's father.

On the walls, in shades of pastel green and timid orange, are small masterpieces by Louis Trézel —the delicate features and intricate folds on his *femmes-fleurs* are equal to Mucha's best work. (The *pâte-de-verre* frescoes by Trézel have often wrongly been attributed to Mucha, but the only establishment in Paris that still boasts works by that famous Czech illustrator is La Crémaillère, in the place du Tertre.)

Just one hundred meters from Brasserie Flo, this former *bouillon* could hardly escape the notice of the acquisitive Jean-Paul Bucher. He imposed his culinary and stylistic prints on it, but managed to leave its identity intact: the contrast is striking between the flickering shadows of Flo and the brilliant light that shines on Julien.

Terminus Nord

23, RUE DE DUNKERQUE, 10TH ARR.

☎ 01 42 85 05 15   🚊 GARE DU NORD

OPEN DAILY FROM 8:00AM UNTIL 1:00AM

THE BRITS ARE IN LUCK. THANKS TO TERMINUS NORD, NOW A VOYAGE THROUGH THE CHUNNEL IS ALMOST LIKE a voyage back in time. As soon as they step off the Eurostar, they can immerse themselves in the timeless food and decor of the Belle Epoque. It's like a remake of *Moulin-Rouge*. The women are no longer wearing hats, and the men stick to today's unassuming ones, but the Terminus Nord still channels that particular ambiance that sets these old train station buffets apart to form their own category among the dynasty of brasseries. Today, without trunks and porters to carry them, elegant women smile through their teeth, with long overcoats hanging from their shoulders, and drag through the station rolling suitcases that threaten the feet of fellow travelers.

The Terminus Nord is a decompression chamber, an opportunity for the culinary re-adaptation to Parisian life. Once you walk through the door, you are greeted, next to a handsome old bar, without undue fanfare, without exaggerated deference — but with a smile befitting a welcome guest.

The currently peaceful coexistence of these two cultures is magnified here: the French journalist embraces his English counterpart; grandmothers pick up grandsons on their way home from an "immersion" in the English language (and still reeling from the

134

charms of the English girls). John pores over the menu, and Jean gives him advice on what to order.

The menu is typical of the Flo group: so, predictable but delectable, and the friend from across the Channel will happily try the *bouillabaisse*, if he hasn't the sense of adventure for the seafood platter.

On the wall, especially in the gorgeous small back room, the high-kitsch frescoes evoke scenes of a lost way of life. In the age of steam trains and private railways, the room belonged to the Northern Railroad Company; if it doesn't quite have the grandiloquent magnificence of Le Train Bleu, it makes up for it by allowing you to pay more attention to your plate than to the ceilings.

On nice days, or in the morning, when the esplanade of the Gare du Nord has been cleared of its nightly wave of suburbanites, take a seat at the small café tables set out on the terrace, and watch the dance of the taxicabs and delivery vans: parting visions of Paris before returning to the mists of Albion.

L'Européen

21 BIS, BOULEVARD DIDEROT, 12TH ARR.

☎ 01 43 43 99 70   🚆 GARE DE LYON

OPEN DAILY FROM 6:30AM UNTIL 1:00AM

WHEN THE BILL WAS STILL PAID IN FRENCH FRANCS, WE CALLED THIS BRASSERIE THE "EURO" AND THE SOUTHERN lilt in our accents would emerge. For visitors from southern France, L'Européen has long functioned as a portal to the capital city: they flocked here for the quintessentially Parisian decor, for a taste of this city via its own particular form of eatery—so particular it had been given a name (brasserie) that didn't exist in Lyon or Marseilles.

At L'Européen, time speeds up, maybe because the clock posted above the bar moves in reverse, as if determined to make you miss your train— or perhaps in a mocking gesture to its sister clock in the belfry of the Gare de Lyon. And indeed, our lilting accents would be all but drowned out in the cheerful din of the dining room—the atmosphere is more muted upstairs—in the constant comings and goings of waiters making their rounds with an alacrity so un-Mediterranean. The most interesting spot was, and remains, the long bar, lined with high-backed stools, where lonely souls or people simply in a hurry eat a solitary lunch, their backs turned to France.

Time passes quickly—and the decor, created by a master of the genre, Slavik, has begun to look a little dated…as have we all. Too much dazzle, perhaps, or too bright in this era of "lounges" with muted, purple walls.

But the Euro has not been devalued: if the history of brasseries has demonstrated anything, it's that styles tend to return...

If the telephone booths (used in a scene shot by Beineix) seem out-of-date now that we all have mobile phones in our pockets, the menu has hardly developed a wrinkle: the seafood sauerkraut remains a must, as does the express lunch menu, often just the thing for someone with a train to catch. But we have retained our weakness for the *coquilles saint-jacques à la provençale*. The quality isn't constant—this is not an exact science—but when they are good, they are surpassingly so. We never had them so good in Provence.

Le Train Bleu

20, BOULEVARD DIDEROT, 12TH ARR.

☎ 01 43 43 09 06   🚆 GARE DE LYON

OPEN DAILY FROM 11:30AM UNTIL 11:00PM

"THERE IS NO MORE BEAUTIFUL RESTAURANT IN ALL OF PARIS THAN THE ONE AT THE GARE DE LYON," DECLARED Louise de Vilmorin, in *The Letter in a Taxi*. For Giraudoux, it was a "hidden museum." Malraux saved it from destruction by getting it added to the national register of historic monuments—the first restaurant to be given the honor—in the early 1970s, when razing old buildings was the order of the day. It is claimed that Salvador Dali was able to live out one of his Surrealist fantasies here: to take a pee while watching trains pull out of a station (this indulgence was unavailable to him at the Gare de Perpignan). Coco Chanel, Colette, Cocteau, Jean Gabin, all would buy platform tickets just to linger at Le Train Bleu.

The buffet at the gare de Lyon was conceived to dazzle visitors to the Universal Exposition of 1900. More than a century later, it still has the power to drop jaws. The decor which was unveiled in 1901 by President Loubet represented a space voyage on the PLM line—the line on which

traveled the famous Train Bleu that inspired Cocteau, Darius Milhaud, Agatha Christie, and John Coltrane. And now, it's also a trek through time. Orientalists Gilbert Galland and Gaston Saint-Pierre, the Marseillan Raymond Allègre, the Sarthois Albert Maignan (to whom we owe the painting of the Théâtre d'Orange, in which Sarah Bernhardt and Réjane appear), the portraitist Guillaume Debufé, the Montpelliérian Max Leenhardt, or even Antoine Calbet (illustrator for Pierre Loti): the creators of the forty-and-one frescoes that adorn the *salle Réjane*, the *salle dorée*, the *salon tunisien*, and the *salon algérien* are more or less forgotten. But the scenes of daily life

in the various cities and towns on the PLM route have kept their charm, thanks to their energy, their colorful naivete, and their old-fashioned realist style.

Le Train Bleu is so beautiful that it's easy to ignore what's happening on your plate—a cuisine well adapted to the environment, reminiscent of the glory days when train food was a world apart from the sandwiches now served by the SNCF.

The specialty of the chef is *escargots de Bourgogne à la chablisienne*. Of course, the decor has its price, which turns up on the bill: a full meal at Le Train Bleu is a first-class ticket.

La Coupole

102, BOULEVARD DU MONTPARNASSE, 14TH ARR.

☎ 01 43 20 14 20　🚇 VAVIN

OPEN DAILY FROM NOON UNTIL 1:00AM,

FRIDAY AND SATURDAY UNTIL 1:30AM

LA COUPOLE IS STILL THAT GIANT PARNASSIAN CANTEEN WHERE YOU'RE LIKELY TO FIND OFF-DUTY JOURNALISTS, elderly couples with a weakness for seafood platters or curried lamb, and someone's cousin from Brittany — not to mention successful authors ready to add their diligence to that of the thirty-two pillars which made the artistic reputation, oft usurped, of this enormous room.

The brouhaha of conversation echoing off the caramel-colored walls and the vastness of the space give only a paltry idea of what La Coupole originally was, even though it has been restored to perfection since it was acquired by Flo in 1988. In 1927, laid off by La Rotonde, which they had been managing, Ernest Fraux and René Lafon decided to hit back. The name, first of all, was meant to taunt the neighboring Rotonde and Dôme. But apart from its insignia, the concept of the place is far from academic. The architects, Barillet and Le Bouc, were ready to indulge the delusions of grandeur of these two Auvergnats: a dance-floor in the basement, a summer restaurant on the first floor, topped by a cupola made of faceted glass. A complex, yes…but not an inferiority complex.

For the decor, the two owners hired the Solvet house, which had already done work at Le Vaudeville and La Closerie des Lilas: The Universal Exposition of 1925 had consecrated the trend toward Art Deco. And so Art Deco would be the house style—big beveled mirrors, crisp clean lines, geometric friezes. And of course, Solvet installed the thirty-two painted pillars that would guarantee the success of this spectacular eatery—and its legend, too. Customers wanted to recognize the brushstrokes of the famous painters who hung around Montparnasse at the time. All Solvet had done was to hire the best students of Matisse and Léger—the reason the pillars were often falsely attributed to them. The proprietors had succeeded in their ruse: soon, La Coupole surpassed the popularity of its neighbors, and thereafter, it continued to evolve with the times. Georges Viaud, former maitre d' and the human memory of the place, smiled when La Coupole aficionados like Phillipe Sollers cried scandal during the 1997 renovation ordered by Jean-Paul Bucher. The owner of the Flo Group did nothing but restore La Coupole to its original state: returning the bar to the left side, giving the plinths back their original color—an olive green that, after the war, had been deemed too reminiscent of German uniforms. Contrary to what the "pillars"—of the establishment, that is, the regulars—believe about the place, this room never stopped evolving, and Georges Viaud even remembers the mildly psychedelic flavor of the central fountain in the 1960s.

Since 1988, La Coupole has supported six floors of office space above its head. Time passes, but its success does not. As for the food, Paul Delbart, now assisted by Romauld Bouvty, continues to provide a solid brasserie-style menu…and a hardworking lamb curry.

Le Dôme

108, BOULEVARD DU MONTPARNASSE, 14TH ARR.

☎ 01 43 35 25 81   🚊 RASPAIL

OPEN DAILY FROM 8:00AM UNTIL 1:30AM

AT THE DÔME, ALL THAT IS LEFT OF THE *MONTPARNOS* WHO USED TO HAUNT THE CARREFOUR VAVIN ARE THEIR graying photos, shrouded in haze and framed in copper, adorning the woodwork at the oldest café in the neighborhood. Montparnasse has settled down, and the Dôme with it: weary of the escapades of a less pleasant bohemian population, it slowly abandoned its former identity, letting go of its café service, then of its strictly brasserie-style menu, to become what it is today—one of the most popular fish restaurants in the city.

So, is it still a brasserie? Yes, given its partiality to fish and seafood, one of the hallmarks of the genre. A deluxe brasserie, where at the tables, beneath colorful curtains installed by Slavik, you'll find executives in suit and tie and hungry young entrepreneurs.

On the menu you'll find *encornets farcis, coquilles saint-jacques*, and line-caught bass. With fish, it all comes down to

a fresh product, perfectly cooked; the Dôme handsomely fulfills these two requirements.

At one table, a group of lively Americans recalls the time when some of their illustrious compatriots made this café their headquarters—along with La Coupole, Le Select, and La Closerie. In the words of Sinclair Lewis, the first American Nobel Prize laureate, from 1930: "Besides all its other advantages, Le Dôme happened to be on a corner that charmingly resembled the corner of Sixth Avenue and Eighth Street in New York, and all the waiters spoke such good English that the customers could remain completely foreign without ever having to resort to Berlitz."

Hemingway, Gertrude Stein, John Dos Passos all slummed it in a Montparnasse that already wasn't what it once was; for the real golden age of Le Dôme was at the very beginning of the century, with Apollinaire and the others who would eventually form the École de Paris after the establishment of La Ruche, on the rue de Dantzig, as a residence house for artists. "This is where we got together, this is where great hopes were born," wrote the neighborhood muse, Kiki, in her memoirs.

Fernand Léger, Matisse, the "customs officer" Henri Rousseau, Marc Chagall, Modigliani, and Foujita; but also Blaise Cendrars and Max Jacob, as well as the less poetic Lenin and Trotsky, spent time at Le Dôme. You could say that it was in this trio of establishments—Dôme, Rotonde, Coupole—bordering the traffic circle of avenue Vavin, that Cubism was born. The Great War put an end to the first party at the Dôme, and the Second World War triumphed over the second wave. In 1953, Kiki died in misery and oblivion, addicted to alcohol and drugs.

The Dôme evolved like the neighborhood did. The Bras family, owners of Zeyer, on the carrefour d'Alésia, acquired it and gave it offspring: Le Bistrot du Dôme, nearby on the rue Delambre; and Le Dôme Bastille, at 2, rue de la Bastille. By the early 1980s, it had definitively moved away from serving drinks and towards becoming the exclusive fish restaurant it is now. But if you walk all the way in the back, to the mahogany bar, you can still recapture a bit of that bygone Parnassian soul—before you return to your table to savor the impeccable risotto of the chef, Franck Graux.

Le Zeyer

234, AVENUE DU MAINE, 14TH ARR.

☎ 01 45 40 43.88 🚇 ALÉSIA

OPEN DAILY FROM 8:00AM UNTIL 12:30AM

LIKE THE WEPLER, ON THE OTHER END OF PARIS, LE ZEYER SERVES AS A PIRATE SHIP, MOORED SEPARATELY FROM the two fleets—bearing the flags of Flo and Blanc—in central Paris. Once, a rumor floated around that the Blanc brothers had incorporated it into their holdings… but it came to nothing. The Zeyer, which belongs to the owners of the Dôme—the very Avey-

ronnais Monsieur and Madame Bras—still waves its own flag, ideally situated between the avenue du Maine and the rue d'Alésia. The only brasserie worthy of the name in the immediate proximity, it is an indispensable meeting place for both business and pleasure. Some celebrities, including Carole Laure, are also regulars.

Those who know the place go to sit upstairs; on their way they'll greet the maitre d', Francis Jammes—a captain and a poet, holding forth from inside his turret in the middle of the ship. It's more convivial up there, and the brasserie atmosphere

gives way somewhat to the spirit of a big provincial restaurant.

Like the Wepler and L'Européen, Le Zeyer is a less pretentious restaurant than many; the decor by Slavik—updated in 1988—has a lot to do with the generous dose of goodwill. And yet, in 1913, when Marcel Zeyer took over the Café de Paris, which used to occupy this spot, he cut the figure of a visionary, an avant-gardist—a trendy designer. Now, it's the faithfulness to his vision that gives Le Zeyer its edge.

Here, as elsewhere, the *plat du jour* is worth your consideration, and the emphasis is on seafood: after all, the navy admiral—Le Dôme— is one of the most sacred seafood restaurants in Paris, and Le Zeyer benefits from the same privileged suppliers. On a recent visit, we had a superb avocado mousse, the most exquisite market-fresh sea snails, and a perfectly cooked *daurade*—also a rarity. The influence of the Alsace is ever-present; the sauerkraut, more worthy than most, pays homage to the original owner, Marcel Zeyer, who had the smart idea to marry the heiress of the Dupont corporation, one of the big names in brasseries at the turn of the century. "It was all good," as the expression goes.

Among the regular customers who have their own napkin rings at the Zeyer, a very few privileged ones had the honor of knowing the Bras family early on, after the War, when Le Zeyer was still a *café-tabac* run by Madame Bras. From the moment it opened, at four o'clock in the morning, the entire fourteenth arrondissement would crowd in to imbibe bowls of *café au lait* and *tartines beurrées*. More than six hundred such bread-and-butter meals were served each day; the early-risers stood ten rows deep.

Le Café du Commerce

51, RUE DU COMMERCE, 15TH ARR.

☎ 01 45 75 03 27 🚇 EMILE-ZOLA

OPEN DAILY FROM NOON UNTIL MIDNIGHT

BRASSERIES ARE TRADITIONAL AFFAIRS, BUT IN THIS EXCEP-TION THAT PROVES THE RULE, THE YOUNG MANAGEMENT team has resolutely turned toward the contemporary. With little touches—*féroce de morue* (a Caribbean dish of mashed cod and avocado with olive oil, pepper, and lemon) appetizer, an astute and daring wine list (Joly, Gramenon)—the Café du Commerce is rewriting the rules of the classic brasserie. The clientele follows suit: the median age is about thirty, and very few of the guests would be able to remember the workers' canteen that occupied this spot before the war.

The mezzanines give the entire place a quasi-Latin feel, and in summer the roof recedes, revealing an unexpected terrace watched over by Marcel Dassault, whose effigy adorns the back wall in homage to the regular column—called "Le Café du Commerce"—the famous aviator and editor ran in his magazine, *Jours de France.*

Like so many of the large spaces that have been converted into modern brasseries, this one had originally been constructed for a less social purpose—it was a big fabric store, converted in 1922 to a canteen for the autoworkers who were omnipresent at Javel. Once nicknamed, a bit pejoratively, "The Thousand Seats," the current café can serve only three hundred diners at a time; it became Le Commerce after the war, taking its inspiration from Chartier.

Reimagined from floor to ceiling when its business began to collapse from fast food competition, it reopened under its new name in 1988. And while the spaciousness and comfort offered by the mezzanines and terrace are the defining charm of this large café, the true connoisseur will prefer to sit downstairs, next to the bar—in view of the bustling wait staff and the playful antics of Étienne Guerraud and his team.

L'Enclos du Temps

31, AVENUE DU MAINE, 15TH ARR.

☎ 01 45 44 52 38 🚇 MONTPARNASSE-BIENVENUE

OPEN MONDAY TO FRIDAY FROM 8:00AM UNTIL 12:30AM,
SATURDAY FROM 10:00AM UNTIL 8:00PM

SEEING BARS EVERYWHERE HE TURNED, XAVIER DE NAMUR DEVELOPED DELUSIONS OF GRANDEUR. YOU COULD COMPARE him to a collector of classic cars…who prefers zinc to chrome, a beer-tap gearshift handle to one made of handworked leather. Already the owner of a half-dozen bistros in the Marais—theme bars, more or less, not without a sense of humor—he added a digit to his favorite arrondissement

to acquire a family station wagon. It's a big, old room slightly below street level at the Gare Montparnasse, on the corner of the avenue du Maine, which unfurls nonchalantly in the shadow of the tower.

In this enclave, shielded from the years, Xavier has bought himself a time machine. L'Enclos du Temps is his invention, from floor to ceiling, created in the great tradition of the Parisian brasserie. Mosaic floor tiles,

nubby leatherette, shining metal bar, wood as polished as the personnel. Everything is faux, and yet the state of mind is perfectly authentic.

The menu is rich, suitable to the means of the chicly disheveled professionals who bustle through at lunchtime, knocking into the café tables strewn on the sidewalk. The *prix fixe* is recommended—it's inventive, and well portioned to prevent the post-lunch fatigue encouraged by the air-conditioned offices in the tower. A charming waitress (who actually smiles!) will present you with your meal, when you're ready…if you're ready… And, the time passes as if Paris was still Paris, as if you could still hail a newsboy or a florist on the street. A short step up, but almost in another world, the cars race around in today's Paris, transplants from Brittany and Bordeaux rush around on the square. The Enclos de Xavier shields you from all of that—for the time it takes to eat a meal.

Le Murat

1, BOULEVARD MURAT, 16TH ARR.

☎ 01 46 51 33 17 🚇 PORTE-D'AUTEUIL

OPEN DAILY FROM 8:00AM UNTIL 12:30AM

THE COSTES DON'T MANAGE BARS, BRASSERIES, OR RESTAU-RANTS—BUT ALL, AND NONE, OF THE ABOVE. THE COSTES manage a concept, a certain idea of being pulled together without seeming so, of being seen while pretending not to care.

And, so…is Le Murat a brasserie? Yes, because it was one before it was re-decorated by Jacques Garcia following the Costes' canon—a neo-Napole-onic style attributed to the emperor's cavalry captain for whom this ultra-trendy establishment is named.

Waistcoats hang from the wall, not from the shoulders of the waiters—who are more likely to be waitresses, very beautiful and distant, if not glacial. The show happens in the dining room—watch for TV personalities—and not on the menu, which offers options about as inventive as a monthly cable plan…though happily the portions aren't as outsized as the bill.

But what does it really matter; you don't come to the Murat to eat Auvergnian sausage and *aligot*. The Costes brothers have demonstrated

that a *bougnat* can be of the times—even ahead of them. Since the opening of the famous Café Costes at Les Halles, a favorite haunt for provincials looking to authenticate their newfound Parisian-ness, their success has not abated.

Like at Café Marly, A la Grande Armée, and Café Ruc, people come here to test their level of notoriety or hipness, and the staff members, recruited more from modeling agencies than from hospitality schools, don't refrain from letting you know their opinion on the matter. But despite everything, the atmosphere at Murat is not unpleasant; it's like the executive club at the international airport. Everything is beautiful—a bit vapid, but relaxed. A little like what you would see on a runway.

Le Congrès Maillot

GÉRARD JOULIE SEEMS TO HAVE MADE A SPECIALTY OF BRASSERIES ON THE PERIPHERY OF PARIS: LE BOEUF Couronné, Le Congrès Auteuil, and this one, at the Porte Maillot, all deliberately sidestep central Paris and offer ideal spots for business lunches or to satisfy a craving for seafood upon emerging from the *periphérique*.

Occupying its spot across from the Palais des Congrès for nearly thirty years, Le Congrès is in a sense the palace of seafood. With Bernard Gonthier—president of the union of fish carvers and a former world champion of fish carving—at the tongs, the restaurant has accustomed its clientele to oysters and crustaceans that are among the finest in all of Paris. *Gillardeau* and *perles blanche* are the stars of an oyster bar featuring twenty varieties.

For those who aren't fans of the sea's offerings, Le Congrès provides other options to appreciate along with its classic, almost clichéd decor —velvet, mirrors, and woodwork—now coming back in fashion. There is a traditional menu offering a *plat du jour* for each day of the week. Lamb is as prized as seafood in this canteen favored by those attending conventions and fairs in the nearby Palais des Congrès as well as residents of Hauts-de-Seine or Yveline who feel no need to descend further into the capital.

A brasserie in the fullest, most traditional sense, accessible and without a false note (without originality, either): it's a safe bet.

La Mascotte

52, RUE DES ABBESSES, 18TH ARR.

☎ 01 46 06 28 15 🚇 ABBESSES, BLANCHE

OPEN DAILY FROM 7:00AM UNTIL 11:30PM

LIKE IT OR NOT, WITH ITS BOASTFUL, OH-SO-PARISIAN MAN-NERISMS, MONTMARTRE WILL NEVER DO ANYTHING like the other "villages" of Paris. And just by virtue of being here during all the mini-revolutions and maxi-tribulations of this little republic-within-the-big-city, La Mascotte has by now indisputably grown into its name. Nothing happens on la Butte without La Mascotte having something to do with it.

Yes, Montmartre has its own brasserie: a Montmartrian brasserie. That is, it's both more and less than a brasserie. In terms of sheer history, it has nothing to envy in its more famous Parisian counterparts. This canteen, which once hosted Jacques Prévert and his *épigones*—make a toast to Andre Grall when you down a beer at the bar—opened in 1889, the same year that the

Eiffel Tower and the Moulin Rouge were built. The Universal Exposition was not for nothing! Ever since then, for more than a century, the exposition continues at the bar, on the faces of the regulars: whether old and wise or young turks, they feast on oysters by the dozen and a glass of Muscadet, all for a trifle.

To be fair, La Mascotte didn't acquire its name until 1934, the date when it resumed its calling as a bistro—after a stint as a theater, which once presented the Edmond Audran operetta for which it was named. Since then, La Mascotte, unlike some of its more goodly sister establishments, has never forgotten that a brasserie is also a place people go to drink.

But let's move into the dining room—and on to more serious things. The essence of a brasserie is eternal, and La Mascotte, managed for some forty years by the Campion family—currently by Thierry—perpetuates it, with its endless display of mirrors and worn leatherette, with its

Auvergnat meat and Breton seafood.

And while the area around Les Abbesses has never been so popular, La Mascotte doesn't bow down to the changing trends: this place is timeless. The proof? The famous transvestite Michou stops by every Sunday at midday to have a drink and listen to the accordion played by one "Florence of Montmartre." Is there a more eternal figure than Michou?

As long as there is La Mascotte, Le Colibri (its sister bar), La Pomponette, La Midinette, and all the dives on the rue Véron, the southern slope of la Butte, will resist, now and forever, the invasion of fleeting fashions.

Wepler

14, PLACE DE CLICHY, 18TH ARR.

☎ 01 45 22 53 29 🚇 PLACE-DE-CLICHY

OPEN DAILY FROM 8:00AM UNTIL 1:00AM

IT ISN'T THE MOST BEAUTIFUL BRASSERIE IN PARIS, NOT THE ONE WHERE YOU'LL EAT THE BEST, BUT THE WEPLER HAS something unique about it, and its devotees are hardcore. Is it the perfect combination of its Alsatian origins and its current Auvergnian management, bringing together the two strongest traditions of Parisian restaurant dining? Or its staunchly Right Bank attitude, far from the snobbery of certain establishments on the other shore? Or its fierce independence in the face of fads and ambitions? The Wepler has its own personality, as attractive today — you may run into members of the young guard of film and literature — as yesterday. Far from the fancier literary bistros of Montparnasse, Henry Miller chose this as his home base: "At one corner of the Place Clichy is the Café Wepler, which was for a long period my favorite haunt. I have sat there inside and out at all times of the day in all kinds of weather. I knew it like a book. The faces of the waiters, the managers, the cashiers, the whores, the clientele, even the attendants in the lavatory, are engraved in my memory as if they were illustrations in a book which I read every day". [*Quiet Days in Clichy*].

The charm of the Wepler depends on the reassuring impression that you are to some extent with family, or at least in a familiar place. The boss, Michel Bessières, and Émile, the oyster shucker, are only part of the cast of characters that will surround you as you work on your seafood platter.

Perhaps the restaurant has also retained—in the patina on its walls—the memories, the laughs, and the chatter of the tea dances that were held here in the 1950s, or the smoky atmosphere of the billiard hall in the adjoining building (now a cinema). Perhaps it's the circa-1935 decor, so cinematographic, that bespeaks an era we would like to have known. Perhaps it's just that the Wepler hasn't sold its soul.

That beautiful fact is everywhere apparent, even in the daring choices of the literary prize that was first given by the Wepler in 2001: a favor returned to the budding authors who have spent so much time at its tables, written their first masterpieces here…and ordered very little.

Au Boeuf Couronné

188, AVENUE JEAN-JUARÈS, 19TH ARR.

☎ 01 42 39 44 44   🚇 PORTE-DE-PANTIN

OPEN DAILY FROM NOON UNTIL 1:00AM

CREATED IN 1865 AT THE SAME TIME AS THE ABATTOIRS OF LA VILLETTE, THIS RESTAURANT—CALLED EDON UNTIL 1932, when it became Au Boeuf Couronné—has survived every war, every fashion, even the move of the meat market to Rungis and the crisis of the mad cow.

Named after an Indian chief, this beautiful brasserie—now across from the Cité de la Musique, which has brought it a new clientele—has earned

the title of "last horse trader in town." Once upon a time, butchers in bloody aprons met here to celebrate the flesh of the cow, the way they once paid homage to the pig at the Cochon d'or, or to the sheep at La Ferme de la Villette (both now gone).

The entire district moved to the rhythms of livestock. On the rue de la Coutellerie, the blades and finely worked handles of the finest, sharpest cooking utensils were proudly displayed. Some vestiges of this time

before the alimentary crises now hang as decoration in the beautiful Art Nouveau dining room of Au Boeuf Couronné. The lustrous woodwork on the wall is as good a reason to visit as the rare steak on the menu.

Those given to nostalgia might claim that said steak isn't as tender or well-seasoned as it once was…but it is the role of nostalgia to exaggerate the merits of the past, while Gerard Joulie's restaurant still offers very choice cuts.

Among the sixteen beef specialties offered—essentially all from the Blond d'aquitaine species—the most spectacular are the *gargantua*, the *pièce charolaise*, and the *côte de boeuf*. But you may prefer the *tartines à la moelle*, accompanied by the *pommes soufflés*, another specialty of the house.

Notes on Artists, Architects, and Decorators

JACQUES GARCIA: The most fashionable decorator in the early 2000s. He renovated Fouquet's, Zimmer, and Le Murat, giving each a touch of youth. A self-made man in the decorative arts, he is also responsible for the interior of Hotel Costes, and has exported his talent as far away as Miami.

JEAN-PIERRE HEIM: Architect, known for his work in the United States. He redesigned the interior at La Lorraine.

LOUIS TRÉZEL: The ceramist hired by the Chartier bothers to take care of the decor at their bouillons. We can thank him for the ceramic murals at the Grand Bouillon Camille Chartier—now Bouillon Racine—and the Grand Bouillon Édouard Chartier, now Montparnasse 1900. Trézel also executed the four Alfred Mucha-inspired *femmes-fleurs* that adorn the walls of the brasserie Julien.

LOUIS MAJORELLE (1859-1926): Woodworker and cabinetmaker. Trained at the Beaux-Arts in Paris, he interrupted his studies to take over the family business, and became one of the most illustrious members of the École de Nancy. He created most of the furnishings in the spectacular brasserie, L'Excelsior, the pride of the *cité lorraine*. In

Paris, he was notably entrusted with the Cuban ebony bar at Julien. His exaggerated ovals, his flower motifs—especially orchids—remain the mark of his workshop, and a characteristic detail of Art Nouveau. He collaborated frequently with the Daum brothers for works involving crystal and stained glass.

CHARLES SPINDLER (1865-1938): Painter and watercolorist. He discovered marquetry in 1893 and became one of the technique's best-known practitioners in France. We are indebted to him for the decor of the brasserie Chez Jenny, and for Bofinger. His studio, now under the direction of his grandson, Jean-Charles, is in the abbey Saint-Leonard, at the foot of the mont Saint-Odile.

SOLVET FRÈRES / SOLVET BROTHERS: School of Art Deco. They decorated Le Vaudeville, La Coupole, and La Closerie des Lilas, among others. Marble columns, wide mirrors in geometric forms, and brightly illuminating wall sconces are their hallmarks.

EDOUARD NIERMANS: Architect, school of Art Nouveau. Among many other successes, he is responsible for the brasserie Mollard, the Hotel Negresco in Nice, and the Hotel de Paris in Monte-Carlo, as well as the Angelina tea salon. With his brother Jean, he also designed the Theatre du Trocadero, the Maison de la Radio, and the Mairie d'Alger.

LÉON FARGUE: Father of the poet Léon-Paul Fargue, ceramist responsible for the faience in the first dining room of the Lipp. His

characteristic style features intricately worked representations of exotic flowers and plants.

LOUIS MADELINE: Architect of Lipp (the second room, in 1925) and of Balzar, also under the direction of the Lipp's owner, Marcelin Cazes.

CHARLES GARREY: Painer, friend of Roland Dorgelès, he painted the African scenes on the ceiling of the Lipp.

SLAVIK: Czech decorator who emigrated to Paris in the 1930s. He became a decorator of the most fashionable restaurants of the 1970s. He brought us Zeyer's new look, and reinvented L'Européen, Le Dôme, and the restaurant at the Eifel Tower. He also helped to salvage Montparnasse 1900.

JEAN-JACQUES WALTZ, OR "HANSIL" (1873-1951): Alsatian painter. He decorated the room in Bofinger that bears his name.

Index

Credits

FRANÇOIS THOMAZEAU is a sports writer, an author of detective novels, and an editor—three professions requiring inspiration and perspiration (and time spent in cafés).

SYLVAIN AGEORGES is a photographer specializing in Paris. He is the author of the *Guide to Jewish-Parisian Heritage* (Éditions Parigramme).

ANNA MOSCHOVAKIS is a poet and translator living in Brooklyn, NY.